SMOKY MOUNTAIN WINES

SMOKY MOUNTAIN WINES

by Paul E. Mahan

arco
New York

Published by Arco Publishing Company, Inc.
219 Park Avenue South, New York, N.Y. 10003

Library of Congress Catalog Card Number 73-78529
ISBN 0-668-03311-8

Printed in United States of America

TO
ALICE

Acknowledgments

My sincere thanks to my many friends, whose names will have to remain anonymous, for allowing me to use their favorite wine recipes. They have been changed only to take advantage of the recent advance and improvements in the art of home winemaking.

A special word of appreciation to Mr. and Mrs. E. J. Arnold, for the privilege of exploring and gathering wild fruits, berries, and flowers from the fields and woods of their farm. Also for the many pleasant hours spent "stalking the wild asparagus" (apology to Euell Gibbons) over the back-country roads and logging trails, here in the mountains, in the farm jeep.

I am indebted to Mr. and Mrs. William Jamison for the many friendly discussions regarding the taste and aroma of the many wines and the merits of the wine materials available here in the Smoky Mountains. Their suggestions and criticisms were invaluable to the completion of this book.

Contents

SMOKY MOUNTAIN WINES

Introduction

Why home winemaking? It is a hobby that can be doubly rewarding. It can turn your leisure time into fun. The double reward comes in consuming the end product.

Recently I picked up a copy of an antique car magazine and noticed that it had a paid subscription of 70,000. Collecting and rebuilding old cars can be a wonderful hobby, providing you are mechanically inclined, have a shop, and several thousand dollars to invest. There are probably millions of hobby winemakers and they need little space and only a few dollars' worth of equipment.

If you live in the country or rural area the source of materials will be no problem. If you live in the city it can be fun, especially if you have children, to drive out into the rural areas looking for wild fruits and berries.

If you locate a berry patch, look up the owner and ask permission to pick some of the fruit. The chances are that he will be glad to give you permission. He will appreciate your courtesy and you will be able to visit there the next season.

The early American colonists made and consumed large quantities of wine. However, wine drinking lost favor and for a time little wine was made and consumed. We turned into a nation of hard liquor and beer drinkers. Wine is making a comeback and there are now many large commercial wineries, especially in California and New York.

Practically all commercial wine is made from grapes. Every state in the United States can grow some variety of grape, and as more wine is consumed more states will become wine producing. However, the home winemaker is not confined only to grapes as winemaking material.

The Great Smoky Mountains of North Carolina are the highest in eastern America and are thought to be the oldest in the world. According to scientists the rock formation at Grandfather Mountain is over a billion years old and supports over 150 varieties of trees. Only one other area, China, surpasses this region in the variety of flowers and trees.

One reason for this wide range of plant life is that during the last Ice Age, which ended some 20,000 years ago, the Great Smoky Mountain area acted as a huge greenhouse where plants survived and developed. Trees like spruce and fir cover many of the mountaintops today. While the area to the north was scoured by great ice sheets, in places over a mile deep, this area escaped and when the ice receded these plants spread out over the eastern United States and Canada.

This great variety of plant life, together with new introductions, makes this area a veritable paradise for the home winemaker. With so many wild fruits, berries, and flowers available as winemaking material, the home winemaker can pursue his hobby throughout the entire year.

ONE

General Information

*Drink no longer water but
use a little wine for thy stom-
ach's sake.*

—1 TIMOTHY 5:23

If you are thinking of joining the growing list of hobby winemakers,
probably the first thought that comes to mind is its legality. It is
legal if you are the head of a household. Before you start, write to
the Department of the Treasury, Internal Revenue Service,
Assistant Regional Commissioner (Alcohol, Tobacco and Firearms)
at the address where you send your income tax statement, and ask
for Form 1541. Fill out and return this form. As the head of a
household, you are permitted to make 200 gallons of wine a year
for your and your family's use, provided the state law does not
prohibit this. There is no charge and no tax connected with this
Form 1541.

Winemaking was an old art in Europe when the first settlers

came to America and found their way into the Great Smoky Mountains. It was only natural that these people brought with them many wine recipes and lost no time in looking around for suitable materials to carry on their winemaking.

Many of the recipes in this book have been handed down through many generations. They have been revised only to take advantage of modern winemaking knowledge and to avoid the hit-and-miss methods of the past.

Only a few years ago the home winemakers faced many problems. The wines they made were of such poor quality that many became discouraged and gave up the hobby, thinking it was impossible to make home wines comparable to commercial kinds.

The mountain people had to use bakers' yeast (or their home-made variety) or else depend on the wild yeasts to ferment their wines. Many wine books written in the past simply gave recipes without giving the reader any knowledge of the modern scientific discoveries that apply to home winemaking today. A wine book that was published only three years ago has over 300 wine recipes, yet none is based on recent winemaking knowledge. Other books are so scientific and detailed regarding the fine points of winemaking that they confuse the beginner. The average home winemaker has neither the time nor the inclination to follow all these details or the money to purchase all the necessary equipment that is needed.

The recipes in this book are based on modern knowledge regarding home winemaking and will produce good wines most of the time. However, there is a wide variation from season to season and area to area in the quality, sugar, and acid content of most fruits so there is bound to be a variation in the quality of wines from one year to the next.

A word of caution to those who intend to gather wild fruits and berries and who are not familiar with the mountains. The Smoky Mountains are also the home of the black timber rattlesnake and the copperhead. The mountainsides that were once farmed have now been abandoned, and many have reverted back to woods and brambles, offering good cover for these reptiles.

While I have gathered all kinds of fruits and berries, and walked through many almost inaccessible places, I have never run across a poisonous snake. However, I have seen several that were killed in the very places I had traveled. The natives here usually wear boots of some kind when picking berries or walking through the woods and undergrowth. They also carry a cane or stick to part the bushes before stepping through them. A good rule to follow is to remember never to put your foot or hand where you cannot see.

During the summer, especially during the hottest part, there are ticks and chiggers. While chiggers won't kill you they can make life uncomfortable for several days after becoming infected with them. Before entering the fields or woods spray your legs and feet with an insect repellent and then take a shower as soon as possible after returning home. Octagon or Fels Naptha soap will remove most of them. There are as many remedies for chigger bites as there are cures for the common cold. I find that a little Sayman's salve rubbed on the spot will relieve the itch and promote healing.

Occasionally one bumps into a hornet's or yellow jacket's nest and if you are allergic to insect stings you should carry bee-sting remedy for such an emergency. For instant relief from bee or wasp stings carry a small bottle of meat tenderizer. Rub a drop on the sting at once. The papain in the meat tenderizer kills the venom injected by the stinger.

Each industry or manufacturing process, over the years, develops words and terms that define each step along the way to the completed product. The wine industry is no exception. Although the terms are numerous, the home winemaker need be familiar with only a few of the terms and abbreviations. Familiarize yourself with the following terms and abbreviations as they will be used throughout the book.

WINE TERMS

Acids. The presence of citric, malic, tartaric, and tannic acids is necessary in the fermenting juice to produce good wines. The recipes recommend the acids needed and the amount.

Dregs. The solids that settle to the bottom of the fermenting vessel during fermentation. The wine term is "lees"; however in this book we will call them sediment.

Fermentation. This is the action that takes place after the yeast has been introduced into the must. The first, or primary, fermentation takes place during the first 3 to 7 days. The secondary fermentation, which is less active, may last from 2 weeks to 3 months.

Fermentation Lock. An apparatus that seals a bottle from the surrounding air but allows the gas (carbon dioxide) created during fermentation to escape.

Must. The name given to the fermenting juice or liquid until fermentation is finished. When fermentation ceases and the liquid is ready to bottle for aging and storing, it is then called wine.

Racking. Pouring or siphoning the must or wine from one vessel to another, leaving behind the sediment in the bottom of the fermenting vessel or bottle.

ABBREVIATIONS

Tsp.	Teaspoon
Tbs.	Tablespoon
Pt.	Pint
Qt.	Quart
Gal.	Gallon
Lb.	Pound
Oz.	Ounce
Pkt.	Packet
Y.N.	Yeast Nutrient
Y.S.	Yeast Starter
A.B.	Acid Blend
A.P.	All Purpose
C.A.	Citric Acid
M.A.	Malic Acid
T.A.	Tartaric Acid

TWO

Equipment

The equipment the home winemaker needs will depend on how much wine he intends to make. It can be as simple or as sophisticated as his pocketbook dictates. If you intend to make your full allotment of 200 gallons you will need more and specialized equipment than if you intend to make only one or two gallons at a time. Here is the equipment you will need as a beginner to make a small amount of wine. Most of it can be found in your own kitchen.

> Enamel saucepan or cooking vessel, 6-qt. size
> Plastic pail or crock, 2-gallon size
> Length of 1/4-inch plastic tubing
> Cheesecloth
> A 1-gallon glass bottle
> Water seal or fermentation lock
> Long-handled wooden spoon
> Several large soft-drink bottles

In the past the home winemaker had to scrounge to find his equipment and he can still do so. If he wishes, however, he can go to a wine supply store and buy manufactured equipment especially made for the purpose. Wine-Art now has stores in many cities. If you do not know of one you can write to the home office, Wine-Art Sales LTD., 3417 West Broadway, Vancouver 8, B.C. Canada for the location of the store nearest you. Many other wine supply houses are advertised in national magazines. The enamel cooking vessel is used for preparing the fruit for fermentation and boiling the sugar to add to the must. It should have a tight fitting lid. Be sure that there are no chips or cracks in the enamel.

The crock or plastic pail is used for fermenting the must or wine. Here in the mountains, most stores and hardware dealers carry the earthenware crocks, in sizes from 1 to 20 gallons. The crocks manufactured today are lighter and safer than the ones manufactured in the past. For fermenting one gallon of wine you need a two-gallon container. If you use plastic for fermenting or handling wine be sure that it is polyethylene, as not all plastics are suitable for winemaking.

The plastic tubing is needed for racking the must and for filling the bottles when the wine has ceased fermentation. You can purchase a siphon with a bulb for starting the flow of liquid at wine supply stores.

The cheesecloth is used to strain the must. Buy the better grade of cheesecloth obtainable at most fabric stores.

The one-gallon glass bottles are used for the secondary fermentation. You can get them almost anywhere. Wine supply stores carry not only these but also cubitainers which come in sizes of 1, 2-1/2, and 5 gallons and are fitted with fermentation locks. They can be folded for easy storage when not in use.

The wooden spoon is used for stirring the must. After fermentation starts wine should NEVER be allowed to come into contact with metal, especially galvanized or copper ware. Contact with metal can cause the wine to have an off flavor. When fermenting fruit pulp, the pulp will rise to the surface of the fermenting vessel and form a compact mass or cap. This needs to be stirred once or twice each day in order to allow more oxygen to get to the yeast. After the pulp has been strained out, the sediment will settle to the bottom and no more stirring is required.

The 28- and 32-ounce throw-away bottles can be used for storing and aging the finished wine. Colored bottles are the best for the finished wine, as wine should not be exposed to light during storage. New screw-on plastic caps are now available at wine supply stores for these bottles. Caps are also available for used liquor bottles as are plastic stoppers and wires for used champagne bottles. Ordinary corks can be used, but with corks it is necessary to store the wine on its side to prevent the corks from drying out.

If you wish to be more scientific in your approach to home winemaking, you can purchase from wine supply stores such equipment as a saccharometer to determine the sugar content and the sugar requirement of the juice used in fermentation. The vinometer is used to determine the alcohol content of wines. The hydrometer determines the specific gravity or density of the juice or must. Printed labels, in color, are available for your bottles, and they add to the pride when serving your finished and aged wine. Let your pocketbook be your guide.

THREE

Materials

Suitable materials for winemaking are almost without limit. Mention was made of the wide variety of plant life in the Great Smoky Mountain area. Here wild fruits, berries, and flowers for making wine are available the year round. Practically all commercial wines are made from grapes, but the home winemaker is not limited to this fruit. Almost any fruit, berries, vegetables, root vegetables, many flowers, grains, and weeds can be used to make delicious wines. The recipes listed in this book use only a few of the many materials available to the home winemaker and are given to fire the imagination of the reader. A brief description and the time of the year that the ingredients are available is given with each recipe.

WATER

Good wine must have good materials. Wine is mostly water, and if you are to have a good wine you must start with good water. The early pioneers built their log cabins near springs, and many of the

13

people living in the mountains today get their water from a spring. Our summer home is built where once the county schoolhouse stood. Our water comes from the same spring from which generations of schoolchildren carried their drinking water, but now it comes to the house through pipes. The water is pure and free of harmful chemicals.

While most city water is safe, it is far from pure. Practically all city water is treated with chlorine and fluorides. According to Daniel E. Okum, Professor of Environmental Health at the University of North Carolina, about half of all Americans whose water is supplied by public service systems are drinking water which "only hours before had been discharged from some industrial or municipal sewer." So if you are in doubt regarding your water, buy deep spring mineral water for your winemaking.

SUGAR

Sugar must be available in any material to cause fermentation and produce wine. Grapes are the only fruit that will make a good wine without the addition of sugar, and only grapes grown in the warm areas of California contain enough sugar. Grapes grown in other parts of the United States require additional sugar. The home winemaker can now buy grape concentrate but the cost per gallon of finished wine will be more than if fresh fruit is used.

The purpose of sugar in winemaking is to produce alcohol. Wine must contain over 10 percent of alcohol by volume in order to preserve it after it is bottled and stored. The winemaker simply creates a suitable atmosphere where yeast, wild or introduced, can act upon the sugar present changing it into alcohol. Fermentation goes on until all the sugar is converted into alcohol or the alcohol content reaches a point where the yeast cannot tolerate any more alcohol and dies, leaving the finished wine.

The amount of sugar to use depends on the type of material used and the kind of wine desired. A dry wine results when all the sugar has been converted to alcohol. A sweet wine results when fermentation stops before all the sugar is converted to alcohol, leaving a residue of sugar in the finished wine.

As a rule 2 to 3 pounds of sugar per gallon will result in a dry wine and 3-1/2 to 4 pounds usually result in a sweet wine. However, this is not always the case, as some yeasts can tolerate more alcohol than others as we shall see when we read about yeasts.

Some wine books, especially those printed in England, call for invert sugar in their recipes. They list the advantages of invert sugar as more smoothness, better flavor, and a saving in time as yeast acts faster on invert sugar. Invert sugar is a liquid and can be bought at some wine supply stores, but your wine will cost more.

You can make invert sugar that will serve the purpose by putting 8 pounds of cane or household sugar in an enameled vessel with 2 pints of water and 1/2 ounce of citric acid. Boil the mixture slowly for 30 minutes, stirring as little as possible. Add enough boiling water to make one gallon. Use at the rate of 1 pint for 1 pound of sugar in any wine recipe. Any not used can be stored in sealed jars, preferably in your refrigerator.

Sugar should be added to the must in stages. Most of the recipes in this book add the sugar in two stages, although many wine books recommend that the sugar be added in three stages. Adding the sugar in stages helps the wine build up a high alcohol content. If you are interested in wine with the highest alcohol content possible, by all means use the three-stage method.

ACIDS

All fruits and vegetables contain certain acids, in varying amounts. A good wine depends, to some degree, on the amount of these acids in the fermenting solution. Many of the mountain people in the past knew nothing and probably never heard the names of the acids in the fruits and vegetables they used. Indeed, it is only recently that the authors of home winemaking books gave the reader some knowledge of the prominent part acids play in winemaking.

While all plants contain acids in their makeup, the acids are not all the same. Apples and blackberries contain mostly malic acid. We know that all citrus fruits contain citric acid. The three acids that are needed in winemaking are citric, malic, and tartaric. All must be present in order to make a good wine. These acids are now available in powder form from your wine supply store. They can be had singly or in a blend of all three. If you know the predominant acid in the fruit you are using, you can then add the others to get the proper acid content in your wine.

Citric acid is the predominant acid in all citrus fruits, currants, elderberries, pears, pineapples, raspberries, and strawberries. Malic acid is the predominant acid in apples, apricots, blackberries, cherries and most plums, peaches, gooseberries, and nectarines. Tartaric acid is found in grapes and raisins.

Rhubarb stalks contain a small amount of oxalic acid, but most of the acid is concentrated in the leaves and roots; otherwise it could not be used as a food. A small amount is harmless; too much would be toxic.

Should the reader care to pursue the subject further, there are wine books that go into detail regarding the acid content and requirements in wines. As a hobby it might be of interest to the home winemaker with a background of science or chemistry, but it is doubtful that the end improvement in the finished wine would justify the added effort.

Wines need a small amount of tannic acid, known in the wine trade as tannin. Only about 1/15th to 1/20th ounce per gallon is needed. Wine without tannin is insipid and lacks "character."

Some fruits like apples and elderberries are high in tannin while others, especially those used in making white wines, are deficient in tannin. Many recipes recommend adding strong tea for its tannin, but there is no way to measure the amount. Grape tannin is available from wine supply stores and it can be measured accurately.

YEASTS

Imagine if you can that one eight-ounce cup of active yeast starter may have 50,000 million active yeast cells. The number of yeast cells that live and die in the making of one gallon of wine is beyond calculation. Even if you had the figures, they would be so long that the mind could not grasp their significance. This will give the winemaker some idea of the importance of yeast.

Books written only a few years ago recommended bakers' yeast in their recipes. It is true that bakers' yeast will cause fermentation and produce wine, however, yeast better suited for winemaking has been discovered and cultivated. It can be bought from wine supply stores. Most recipes here call for Andovin all-purpose wine yeast. This yeast not only tolerates a higher degree of alcohol, but also settles to the bottom and clings there, making it easier to strain or siphon without getting any of the dregs in your finished wine.

The wine yeast most home winemakers use comes in the form of dry granules in sealed packets. Each packet contains enough yeast to activate 5 to 8 gallons of must. One-fourth teaspoon is enough for 1 gallon.

The yeast can be introduced into the must by sprinkling the dry yeast over the top of the must. However, there is a better and more efficient way which is known as the yeast starter. Two types of starter are used in this book.

The first is the juice starter. When fruit juice is being fermented, take one cup of the juice and put it in a small enamel pan. Add one tablespoon of sugar, bring it to a boil, and boil for 2 minutes. Pour the mixture into a sterilized jar and allow it to cool. Now add one-fourth teaspoon of yeast nutrient and one-fourth teaspoon of yeast for each gallon of must to be fermented. Cover with a piece of plastic wrap and secure with a rubber band. Let it stand in a warm place for 12 to 24 hours.

The second is the orange juice starter. Take one-fourth to one-half cup of orange juice and enough water to make one cup and proceed as for the juice starter.

By using the starter, instead of sprinkling a few dry granules of yeast on top of the must and waiting two or more days for it to begin action, you now introduce millions of active yeast cells; fermentation will begin in a matter of hours.

Bakers' yeast can be introduced by spreading it on a slice of toasted bread. Mix the yeast in a little boiled and cooled water to a paste and spread it on the toast. Place the toast, yeast side down, on top of the must. Remove the toast after fermentation starts.

If you are making several batches of wine a few days apart, you can stretch the starter by leaving one-fourth cup in the jar and adding more juice, sugar, and nutrients. You can also use the yeast or sediment left in the fermenting vessel to start another batch of wine; however, it is best to use this but once. The yeast starter can be kept for several weeks in the refrigerator and reactivated by adding a little sugar syrup and placing it in a warm place.

Besides the all-purpose yeast there are available special yeasts such as champagne, port, and sherry. If you use honey there is a special yeast for that purpose called mead yeast.

NUTRIENTS

Yeast, to work efficiently, needs certain nutrients. Some are present in the fermenting solution and others need to be added by the winemaker. The main nutrient needed is ammonium phosphate. It can be had from wine supply stores in powder form or in nutrient tablets. Vitamin B_1, while not absolutely necessary, will help speed fermentation. When making honey wines a pinch of Epsom salts (magnesium sulphate) can be added. Root wines will benefit by the addition of a few Vitamin C tablets; however, be sure they are from a natural source and not synthetic.

CAMDEN TABLETS

The early mountain people made their wines by placing the fruit or berries in a crock or wooden cask and then letting nature take over the fermenting. Many of their wines would eventually sour and turn to vinegar, which accounts for their calling wine "sour water." The term can still be heard when talking to the older generation of mountain people. Many made their own yeast or used bakers' yeast.

Wild yeasts are everywhere. They are on the fruit and berries in the form of molds. They are in the air along with dusts. If left uncovered, the vinegar fly will infect the fruit or must.

The problem that faces the home winemaker is how to destroy these undesirable yeasts and bacteria before introducing the cultivated kind. The mountain people had but one method: to boil the fruit or juice, although boiling changed the flavor and destroyed the delicate aroma of many fruits. Now the chemist has come to the rescue with the camden tablet (sulfur dioxide).

Camden tablets added to the juice or crushed fruit at the rate of 1 tablet to 1 gallon of juice or fruit and left for 24 hours will destroy all foreign yeasts and bacteria. This method is called sulfiting the must.

Dissolve 1 camden tablet in one-half cup of boiled and cooled water for each gallon of juice or fruit. Stir it into the must and allow it to stand for 24 hours. Stir two or three times during this period. The must should be tightly covered at all times, except when stirring or racking.

Some wine materials, such as root vegetables, require boiling. This is explained in the chapter on root wines.

FOUR

Fruit Wines

Some of the fruits mentioned in this chapter are native to this area; others were planted by the early settlers. Although the favorite American dessert is apple pie, apples are not native to America. The origin of the apple is hidden in the shadows of the past, prior to recorded history. The Romans are thought to have introduced them into England and the early English settlers brought them to America.

We have all read the story about Johnny Appleseed (John Chapman), the traveling preacher, who preached the gospel on Sunday and planted apple orchards along his trail during the week. The Indians, as they were forced to move ever farther west, scattered apple seeds, and when the settlers followed they found apple trees growing along their trails. Today the United States is the greatest apple-producing country in the world.

Apple seeds do not produce true to the parent tree. Each seed planted will differ from other seeds from the same tree and be different from the parent tree. Many of our old standby varieties were found by chance. The winesap was found growing in the woods of Rhode Island; the delicious in a pasture in Iowa.

Back when the country was young, most of the apples grown in our country went into the production of cider. However, there came a time when the apple industry was threatened with extinction. The original settlers, even the preachers and religious groups, were fond of their hard cider. Their glasses or mugs were quart-size. Then somebody made the discovery that alcohol was sinful and the work of the devil. The temperance movement, like a blight, spread over the land. Farmers chopped down their apple trees or let their orchards decay. Cellars no longer had hogsheads of hard cider to entertain company.

However, some enterprising farmer who had kept his apple trees discovered that apples were good to eat as well as drink. He coined the slogan, "An apple a day keeps the doctor away," to sell his apples, and saved the apple industry.

The early mountain people wasted nothing in the way of food. When they prepared apples for drying or for apple butter they saved the peelings. They dried them slightly in the sun or on the back of the stove, and made an apple beer with them. They placed the peelings in a crock, covered them with boiling water, sometimes adding a little sugar, and let them set for a few days, until the flavor came out and fermentation started. Back in those days there were no poison sprays to worry about.

While visiting in Pennsylvania I saw hundreds of acres, once thriving farms, now grown up in wild apples. The seeds scattered by grazing cattle and deer have now taken root to bring forth apples of many sizes, colors, and flavors. Wild apples are found growing throughout the mountains and many are excellent for wines. While most home winemakers will have to settle for store-bought apples we here in the mountains have a wide choice of wild apples to use in our winemaking.

Two recipes are given here but there are many more variations. The home winemaker can let his imagination run wild and perhaps find a new or better recipe to capture the taste and aroma of ripe apples in a good wine.

APPLE WINE — PULP METHOD

10 lbs. apples
4 lbs. sugar
2 oranges
4 oz. raisins

1 tsp. Y.N.
5 qts. water
Orange A.P. Y.S.

Wash the apples thoroughly but do not peel. Cut them in half and remove the core. Slice the rest of the apples into a fermenting vessel and pour 3 qts. boiling water on them and allow to cool. Add 1 camden tablet that has been dissolved in a little boiled and cooled water. Allow to stand for 24 hours, stirring two or three times. Wash the oranges and dip them into boiling water for a few seconds. With a sharp knife cut off a thin strip of the peel, being careful not to cut off any of the white pith. Twist the peel to release the oil and drop it into the must. Cut away all the white pith and discard it along with the seeds. Slice the rest into the must. Add the Y.N. and the chopped raisins. Boil one-half of the sugar in 1 qt. of water for 2 minutes and when cool add to the must. Introduce the yeast starter and ferment for 5 days. Strain out the solids. Boil the rest of the sugar in the rest of the water for 2 minutes and when cool add to the must. Ferment for 10 days, siphon into a 1 gal. glass bottle, and fit with a fermentation lock.

APPLE CIDER WINE

3 qts. apple cider
4 lbs. sugar
1 tsp. A.B.

1 tsp. Y.N.
2 pts. water
Juice A.P. Y.S.

Pour the apple cider into a fermenting vessel and add the A.B., Y.N., and 1 camden tablet that has been dissolved in a little boiled and cooled water. Allow to stand for 24 hours, stirring two or three times. Boil one-half of the sugar in 1 pt. of water for 2 minutes and when cool add to the must. Introduce the yeast starter and ferment for 5 days. Siphon the must into another sterilized fermenting vessel, leaving behind as much of the sediment as possible. Boil the rest of the sugar in the rest of the water for 2 minutes and when cool add to the must. Ferment for 10 days, siphon into a 1 gal. glass bottle, and fit with fermentation lock.

Note: If you use pasturized apple juice it will not be necessary to add the camden tablet.

CHERRY

Cherries make excellent wines. The early settlers planted both the red and the black, and some of the trees are still growing where homesteads were located. The dark sweet cherry makes an excellent sweet wine, but the fresh fruit is hard to find on the market. The recipe that follows uses the canned fruit.

The wild black cherry is scattered throughout the mountain forests. Many trees are found along highways and streams. The fruit of the wild cherry ripens in August and early September.

SOUR RED CHERRY WINE

6 lbs. cherries	1/4 tsp. tannin
2 lbs. sugar	7 pts. water
1 tsp. Y.N.	Juice A.P. Y.S.

Remove the seeds, place the cherries in a fermenting vessel and crush them. Add 5 pts. of boiled and cooled water, Y.N., tannin, and 1 camden tablet that has been dissolved in a little boiled and cooled water. Let stand for 24 hours, stirring two or three times. Boil one-half the sugar in 1 pt. water for 2 minutes and when cool add to the must. Ferment for 10 days, siphon into a 1 gal. glass bottle, and fit with a fermentation lock.

DARK SWEET CHERRY WINE

4 1-lb. cans dark cherries
2 lbs. sugar
Juice of 2 oranges

1 tsp. Y.N.
1 qt. water
1/2 tsp. A.P. yeast

Empty the contents of the cans into a fermenting vessel, add the orange juice, Y.N., and sprinkle the dry yeast over the top. Allow to ferment for 5 days, stirring once each day. Strain out the solids and wring dry. Boil the 2 lbs. sugar in 1 qt. of water for 2 minutes and when cool add to the must. Ferment for 10 days, siphon into a 1 gal. glass bottle, and fit with a fermentation lock.

WILD CHERRY WINE

1 gal. cherries
3 lbs. sugar
Juice of 2 lemons
4 oz. chopped raisins

1 tsp. Y.N.
4 qts. water
Juice A.P. Y.S.

Place the cherries in a fermenting vessel and crush them, being careful not to crush any of the seeds. Add 2 qts. of boiled and cooled water, Y.N., lemon juice, and 1 camden tablet that has been dissolved in a little boiled and cooled water. Let stand for 24 hours, stirring two or three times. Boil 2 lbs. of the sugar in 1 qt. of water for 2 minutes and when cool add to the must. Introduce the Y.S. and ferment for 2 days. Strain out the solids. Add the chopped raisins and ferment for 5 days. Boil the rest of the sugar in the rest of the water and when cool add to the must. Ferment for 10 days, siphon into a 1 gal. glass bottle, and fit with a fermentation lock.

PERSIMMON

The persimmon that grows here in the mountains is small and requires one or more heavy frosts to ripen. The mountain people made persimmon wine by gathering the fruit after a good frost. They used a barrel with a spigot in the bottom. First they placed a layer of straw and then a layer of persimmons. This was repeated until they filled the barrel or ran out of fruit. Natural fermentation began and the wine was run off the bottom from the spigot.

PERSIMMON WINE

2 lbs. ripe persimmons	1 tsp. Y.N.
3 lbs. sugar	4 qts. water
4 oz. chopped raisins	Orange A.P. Y.S.

Put the fruit and chopped raisins in a fermenting vessel and crush them. Add three qts. of boiled and cooled water and 1 camden tablet. Allow to stand for 24 hours, stirring two or three times. Add the Y.N. Boil one-half of the sugar in 1 pt. of water for 2 minutes and when cool add to the must. Introduce the Y.S. and ferment for 5 days, stirring once each day. Strain out the solids. Boil the rest of the sugar in the rest of the water for 2 minutes and when cool add to the must. Ferment for 5 days, siphon into a 1 gal. glass bottle, and fit with a fermentation lock.

PEACH

Someone walking through a field or woods eating a peach throws the pit away. Some fall on fertile ground and take root, and another peach tree grows to bring forth fruit of its kind. However, like many other varieties of fruit, they do not come true to the parent tree, so another variety of wild peach grows. These wild peaches, if you can find them, make an excellent wine. Most of our commercial peaches are bred for looks, and aroma and flavor are sacrificed in the process.

PEACH WINE

10 lbs. peaches
3 lbs. sugar
1 pkt. dried elder flowers
1 tsp. A.B.

1 tsp. Y.N.
1/4 tsp. tannin
4 qts. water
Orange A.P. Y.S.

Wash the peaches in running water but do not peel. Slice the peaches into a fermenting vessel and toss in the pits. Add 2 qts. of boiled and cooled water, A.B., Y.N., tannin, and 1 camden tablet. Let stand for 24 hours, stirring two or three times. Boil one-half of the sugar in 1 qt. of water for 2 minutes and when cool, add to the must. Introduce the yeast starter and ferment for 3 days. Strain out the solids and add the elder flowers. Ferment for 5 days and strain out the solids. Boil the rest of the sugar in the rest of the water for 2 minutes and when cool add to the must. Ferment for 10 days, siphon into a 1 gal. glass bottle, and fit with a fermentation lock.

PEARS

Pears make a light table wine. The sand pear has been growing in the southern states for many generations. Some trees that are still growing are perhaps over a hundred years old. The fruit is rock hard and never softens for eating out of hand. They are used for canning and preserves, and make a good wine.

SAND PEAR WINE

10 lbs. sand pears
3-1/2 lbs. sugar
4 oz. chopped raisins
1 tsp. A.B.

1 tsp. Y.N.
1/4 tsp. tannin
5 qts. water
Orange A.P. Y.S.

Cut the pears in half, remove the seeds and cut off the ends. Slice the pears into an enamel pan and add 3 qts. of water. Simmer for 30 minutes. Put 1-1/2 lbs. of the sugar and the chopped raisins in a fermenting vessel, strain the juice from the pears over them, and discard the pulp. Stir until the sugar is dissolved. When cool add the A.B., Y.N., tannin, and introduce the yeast starter. Ferment for 3 days. Boil 1 lb. of sugar in 1 pt. of water for 2 minutes and when cool add to the must. Ferment for 5 days and then carefully siphon into another fermenting vessel, leaving behind as much of the sediment as possible. Boil the rest of the sugar in 1 pt. of water for 2 minutes and when cool add to the must. Ferment for 5 days, siphon into a 1 gal. glass bottle, and fit with fermentation lock.

PLUMS

Plums come in many sizes, colors, and flavors. The greengage and blue damson are old-time favorites. Here in the mountains a wild plum grows along the creeks and in damp locations that the natives call the "hog plum." (It must be called so because they are so sour that only a hog can eat them.) The tree has a black bark and the branches are covered with many thorns. In the spring, however, the snow-white blossoms make the tree look as though it were covered with cotton fluff. Hog plums ripen in August and make a strong table wine.

HOG PLUM WINE

5 lbs. plums   4 qts. water
3-1/2 lbs. sugar   Juice A.P. Y.S.
1 tsp. Y.N.

Put the plums into a fermenting vessel and crush them, being careful not to crush any of the pits. Add 3 qts. of boiled and cooled water and 1 camden tablet. Let stand for 24 hours, stirring two or three times. Boil 2 lbs. of the sugar in 1 pint of water and when cool add to the must. Add the Y.N. and introduce the yeast starter. Ferment for 2 days, strain out the solids, and discard. Ferment for 5 days. Boil the rest of the sugar in the rest of the water for 2 minutes and when cool add to the must. Ferment for 5 days, siphon into a 1 gal. glass bottle, and fit with fermentation lock.

DAMSON PLUM WINE

8 lbs. plums	4 qts. water
3 lbs. sugar	Juice A.P. Y.S.
1 tsp. Y.N.	

Follow the same method as for Hog Plum Wine.

RED PLUM WINE

8 lbs. red plums	4 qts. water
3 lbs. sugar	Juice A.P. Y.S.
1 tsp. Y.N.	

Follow the same method as for Hog Plum Wine.

ROSE HIPS

Some varieties of roses after they bloom form small hard fruits called hips. In the fall of the year when they mature they can be gathered to make a beautiful and excellent light pink wine. Rose hips are used commercially to produce Vitamin C and are available in both ground and powder forms at health food stores. Most rose hips used are imported from Europe. Rosa Rogusa and Rosa Setigern both form hips and are found growing in the mountains, the first around old homesites and the latter growing wild.

ROSE HIP WINE

3 lbs. whole rose hips or   Scented rose petals
   2 lbs. ground   Orange sherry Y.S.
3 lb. sugar   5 qts. water
4 oz. sultana raisins

If you gather the wild hips you will have to wait until fall when they are ripe. If you purchase the hips you can make the wine any time during the year. A pint of scented rose petals will give the wine an aroma, but they are not necessary.

If whole hips are used, first wash them in one-half gallon of water in which 1 camden tablet has been dissolved. Sterilize the food mill or blender by rinsing it out with a little of the camden water and then with a little boiled water. Grind or chop the hips and put them into a fermenting vessel. Put in the petals, if used, raisins and one-half of the sugar in an enamel pan and add 3 qts. water. Bring to a boil and boil for 2 minutes. Pour over the hips, cover, and allow to cool. Introduce the yeast starter and ferment for 5 days, stirring once each day. Strain out the solids and discard. Boil the rest of the sugar in the rest of the water for 2 minutes and when cool add to the must. Ferment for 5 days, siphon into a 1 gal. glass bottle and fit with a fermentation lock.

If you buy ground hips, place the hips, chopped raisins, and petals in a fermenting vessel, add 1 camden tablet and let stand for 24 hours. Proceed as above.

FIVE

Berry Wines

There are many more species of berries that grow in the Smoky Mountains than the ones used in the following recipes. I am acquainted with the flowering red raspberry, but was surprised to learn that there is a red raspberry that grows on Clingman's Dome above 6,000 feet. It grows among the rocks and ripens in August and early September. There are several varieties of dewberries, whose vines trail on the ground, and even a thornless blackberry. There are also the barberry, chokeberry, coralberry, deerberry, hackberry, and mountain cranberry, just to name a few of them.

BLACKBERRY

Blackberry wine is so popular here in the mountains because of the abundance of the berries. They are still to be found growing wild, especially in abandoned fields and on mountainsides. When a farm field is abandoned, blackberry vines are the first to take over; then softwood trees like the tulip poplar spring up, only in time to be crowded out by the hardwood trees. That is nature's way of reclaiming her land. It is a beautiful sight in early June when the roadsides and fields are white with blackberry blossoms. Beginning about the fourth of July the berries start turning red and then black and ripe.

Blackberries lend themselves to many types of good wines. Our first recipe is for a light dry table wine.

DRY BLACKBERRY WINE

5 lbs. blackberries   1/4 tsp. tannin
3 lbs. sugar   7 pts. water
Juice of 2 lemons   Juice A.P. Y.S.
1 tsp. Y.N.

Use only fully ripe berries. This is important, as only a few green or partly ripe berries can change the flavor of the finished wine. The berries should be picked on a sunny day after the dew has dried. Put the berries in an enamel pan and crush them. Add 2 qts. of water that has been boiled and cooled and 1 camden tablet. Let stand for 24 hours, stirring two or three times. Strain the juice into a fermenting vessel and discard the pulp. Add the lemon juice, Y.N., and tannin. Boil one-half of the sugar in 1 qt. of water for 2 minutes and when cool add to the must. Introduce the Y.S. and ferment for 5 days. Siphon into another fermenting vessel, leaving behind as much of the sediment as possible. Boil the rest of the sugar in 1 pt. of water for 2 minutes and when cool add to the must. Ferment for 10 days, siphon into a 1 gal. glass bottle, and fit with a fermentation lock.

Blackberries being the most plentiful of berries, the following recipe is for 5 gallons. The amount of water used will depend on the juiciness of the berries, as some varieties contain more juice than others. When the last of the sugar is added it can be determined how much water needs to be added in order to make 5 gallons.

SWEET PORT-STYLE BLACKBERRY WINE

40 lbs. blackberries   1/2 tsp. tannin
20 lbs. sugar   7 qts. water
 6 oranges   Juice A.P. Y.S.
 1 pkt. Y.N.

Crush the berries a few pounds at a time and pour them into a fermenting vessel. Add 1 gal. of water that has been boiled and cooled. This should make about 4 gals. in the fermenting vessel. Add 4 camden tablets and let stand for 24 hours, stirring two or three times. Boil 5 lbs. of sugar in 1 qt. of water for 2 minutes and when cool add to the must. Add the Y.N., tannin, and introduce the Y.S. Ferment for 2 days after fermentation starts and then strain out the solids and discard. Dip the oranges into boiling water for a few seconds. With a sharp knife cut off a thin slice of the peel, being careful not to cut off any of the white pith. Twist or bruise the peel, to release the oil and drop it into the must. Cut away all the white pith and discard it along with the seeds. Slice the rest of the orange into the must. Boil 5 lbs. of sugar in 1 qt. of water for 2 minutes and when cool add to the must. Ferment for 5 days and then boil another 5 lbs. of sugar in 1 qt. of water for 2 minutes, and when cool add to the must. Ferment for 5 days and strain out the solids, being careful to leave as much of the sediment behind as possible. Boil the rest of the sugar in enough water to make 5 gallons in the fermenting vessel. When cool add it to the must and ferment for 10 days. Siphon into a 5 gallon cubitainer or glass bottles and fit with fermentation locks.

BLUEBERRY

There are several varieties of wild blueberries that grow here in the mountains. One, the highbush, is the parent of most of the cultivated varieties. The bushes grow from 3 to 10 feet high. The plant prefers moist locations. The fruit, blue to bluish black, is sweet and juicy. However, some bushes, for some reason, have sour fruit. The fruit ripens from June through early August and makes a good dry or sweet wine.

WILD BLUEBERRY WINE

1 gal. blueberries	1/4 tsp. tannin
3 lbs. sugar	4 qts. water
1 tsp. A.B.	Juice A.P. Y.S.
1 tsp. Y.N.	

If you are picking the wild blueberries, it is best to sample a berry to make sure you are getting the sweet kind. Put the berries in a fermenting vessel and crush them. Add 2 qts. of water that has been boiled and cooled, A.B., Y.N., and 1 camden tablet. Allow to stand for 24 hours, stirring two or three times. Boil one-half of the sugar in 1 qt. of water for 2 minutes and when cool add to the must. Introduce the Y.S. and ferment for 2 days. Strain out the solids and discard. Boil the rest of the sugar in 1 qt. of water for 2 minutes and when cool add to the must. Ferment for 10 days, siphon into a 1 gal. glass bottle, and fit with a fermentation lock.

BUCKBERRY — HUCKLEBERRY

While the plants and fruit of these two berries resemble the blueberry, they belong to different plant families. The buckberry and huckleberry belong to Gaylussacia and the blueberry belongs to the Vaccinium plant family. The buckberry is endemic to the southern Appalachian Mountains, while the huckleberry grows from Canada to Florida. The buckberry prefers the shade of the oak and chestnut and may cover an entire mountain top. The huckleberry grows in less shade and in the open near the woods. Huckleberries grow on short bushes some not over a foot high. They are mean to gather. The best way is to pick all the berries on a bush and then pick them over later. Spread the berries out in a shallow pan and pick out all the trash and green berries. The buckberry is sour and high in pectin. The huckleberry is sweet when ripe. Both make good wine, although care must be exercised when making wine with the buckberry not to release too much pectin, or the wine will not clear and will have a pectin haze.

LIGHT DRY BUCKBERRY WINE

3 lbs. buckberries
2-1/2 lbs. sugar
2 tsp. Y.N.

1/4 tsp. tannin
4 qts. water
Juice A.P. Y.S.

Put the berries in an enamel pan and crush them. Add 3 qts. of water that has been boiled and cooled, and 1 camden tablet. Let stand for 24 hours, stirring two or three times. Strain the juice into a fermenting vessel and discard the pulp. Add the Y.N. and tannin. Boil 1-1/2 lbs. of the sugar in 1 pt. of water for 2 minutes and when cool add to the must. Introduce the Y.S. and ferment for 5 days. Siphon into another fermenting vessel, leaving behind all the sediment. Boil the rest of the sugar in 1 pt. of water and when cool add to the must. Ferment for 5 days, siphon into a 1 gal. glass bottle, and fit with a fermentation lock.

LIGHT DRY HUCKLEBERRY WINE

1 gal. huckleberries
3 lbs. sugar
1 tsp. A.B.
1 tsp. Y.N.

1/4 tsp. tannin
4 qts. water
Juice A.P. Y.S.

Put the berries into a fermenting vessel and crush them. Add 2 quarts of boiled and cooled water, A.B., tannin, and 1 camden tablet. Allow to stand for 24 hours, stirring two or three times. Boil one-half of the sugar in 1 qt. of water for 2 minutes and when cool add to the must. Ferment for 5 days, then strain out the solids, and discard. Boil the rest of the sugar in the rest of the water for 2 minutes and when cool add to the must. Ferment for 10 days, siphon into a 1 gal. glass bottle, and fit with a fermentation lock.

GOOSEBERRY

The mountain people at one time had patches of gooseberries and currants growing near their homes. They have long since died out and the North Carolina State Plant Board does not allow these plants to enter the state now. These plants act as alternate host plants to the white pine blister disease.

However, there is a wild fruit that grows here in the mountains that the natives call gooseberries. While the fruit resembles the gooseberry it belongs to the blueberry family of plants. They are listed in plant books under the name "deerberry." They grow in the shade of trees in the woods or in fields close to the woods. The fruits are greenish to pale purple and drop off the bush soon after ripening. The best way to gather them is to spread a cloth under the bush and shake the berries onto the cloth. They make a good dry wine. The fruit ripens during late August and September.

GOOSEBERRY WINE

5 lbs. gooseberries   1 tsp. A.B.
3 lbs. sugar   5 qts. water
1 tsp. Y.N.   Orange A.P. Y.S.
1/4 tsp. tannin

Use berries that show some color. Follow the same method as for elderberries, but let the berries ferment for 5 days before straining out the pulp.

JUNEBERRY

The juneberry, serviceberry, or sarvisberry perhaps should be included in fruit wines as it grows on trees. The tree, the common Allegheny serviceberry, grows here in the mountains up to the 6,000 foot elevation. The fruit is small and about the color and size of cranberries. It is sweet and makes a good sweet wine. The berries ripen in June, hence the name juneberry.

JUNEBERRY WINE

3 lbs. juneberries   1 tsp. Y.N.
4 lbs. sugar   7 pts. water

4 ozs. raisins   Orange A.P. Y.S.
1 tsp. A.B.

Put the fruit in a fermenting vessel and crush it. Add 2 qts. of
water that has been boiled and cooled, the A.B., Y.N., and 1
camden tablet. Let stand for 24 hours, stirring two or three times.
Boil one-half of the sugar in 1 qt. of water for 2 minutes and then
cool and add to the must. Introduce the Y.S. and ferment for 2
days. Strain out the solids. Add the chopped raisins and ferment
for 5 days. Boil the rest of the sugar in the rest of the water and
when cool add to the must. Ferment for 10 days, siphon into a 1
gal. glass bottle, and fit with a fermentation lock.

ELDERBERRY

The black and red elderberry grow here in the mountains. The
black-berried elderberry prefers a moist location and can be found
growing along the small streams and fence rows. The fruit ripens
in August and early September.

The red-berried elderberry is found growing up to 4,000 feet. It
blooms and ripens earlier; the peak at the higher altitudes is July.
At lower elevations it may ripen as early as May.

Both the fruit and blossoms can be used to make excellent wines.
Elderberry blossom wine has been made and drunk for centuries.

SWEET PORT-STYLE
ELDERBERRY WINE

5 lbs. elderberries   1 tsp. Y.N.
4 lbs. sugar   7 pts. water
1 tsp. A.B.   Juice A.P. Y.S.

Use only fully ripe berries. Wash them by swishing handfuls of berries in a pail of water. Shell the berries from the stems, being careful to remove all the bits of stems. Place the berries in a fermenting vessel and crush them. Add the A.B., Y.N., 5 pts. of water that has been boiled and cooled, and 1 camden tablet. Let stand for 24 hours, stirring two or three times. Boil 2 lbs. of the sugar in 1 pt. of water for 2 minutes and when cool add to the must. Introduce the Y.S. and ferment for 2 days. Strain out the solids. Ferment for 5 days. Boil the rest of the sugar in 1 pt. of water and when cool add to the must. Ferment for 10 days, siphon into a 1 gal. glass bottle, and fit with a fermentation lock.

MULBERRY

The mulberry tree is scattered through the mountains. When the tree grows in the open it has low spreading branches. When it grows in the forest it grows tall. There are several varieties: black, red, and white. There is also a weeping mulberry that is not very common; the branches grow down instead of up. When the tips of the branches reach the ground they take root. The fruit of the trees that grow wild are small, and when ripe, mild and sweet. The mulberry makes a good sweet wine. It can be combined with rhubarb to make a good mixed wine.

MULBERRY WINE

5 lbs. mulberries	1/4 tsp. tannin
4 lbs. sugar	4 qts. water
1 tsp. A.B.	Orange A.P. Y.S.
1 tsp. Y.N.	

Follow the same method as for Blackberry Wine.

WILD BLACK RASPBERRY

The wild raspberry, like the wild strawberry, has a delightful aroma. It is found growing throughout the mountains, but only a few are found growing in one place. They prefer the more inaccessible locations like a rock cliff or a rocky spot on steep mountainsides. They are also found along fence rows and county roads. It takes a lot of scrounging to come up with a gallon of these berries, but the delightful flavor and aroma in a wine makes the search worthwhile. They will make either a dry or a sweet dessert wine. The recipe here is for a sweet wine; for a dry wine reduce the sugar to 2-1/2 pounds. The berries ripen in June, just before the blackberries.

SWEET WILD BLACK RASPBERRY WINE

4 lbs. berries	1 tsp. A.B.
3-1/2 lbs. sugar	7 pts. water
8 oz. raisins	Juice A.P. Y.S.
1 tsp Y.N.	

Follow same method as for Blackberry Wine, except use 1-1/2 lbs. sugar to start fermentation.

RED RASPBERRY (CULTIVATED)

There are two varieties of red raspberries that grow wild here in the mountains. They cannot be found in quantity enough to make a wine, so we will have to settle for the cultivated which can be found at the markets and fruit stands in June. If you find a supply you will find the cost is worthwhile as they make a beautiful light red wine that has a tantalizing aroma and taste.

RED RASPBERRY WINE

4 lbs. red raspberries	4 oz. sultana raisins
4 lbs. sugar	4 qts. water
1 tsp. A.B.	Juice A.P. Y.S.
1 tsp. Y.N.	

Follow the same method as for Blackberry Wine.

WILD STRAWBERRY

Wild strawberries with that tantalizing aroma and taste grow everywhere here in the mountains. Any place the sun can get through the shade of the trees you will find wild strawberries growing. It is worth all the tedious work of picking and stemming these little gems of goodness to capture their taste and aroma in a sweet wine.

Within that small globe is all the fragrance and essence of a perfect June day. You can find the ripe fruit from the middle of May through most of June.

SWEET WILD STRAWBERRY
DESSERT WINE

4 lbs. wild strawberries	1 tsp. Y.N.
4 lbs. sugar	7 pts. water
4 oz. raisins	Juice A.P. Y.S.
1 tsp. A.B.	

Put the berries in an enamel pan or plastic pail and crush them. Add 5 pts. of water that has been boiled and cooled and 1 camden tablet. Let stand for 24 hours stirring two or three times. Strain the juice into a fermenting vessel and discard the pulp. Add the chopped raisins, A.B., and Y.N. Boil 2 lbs. of the sugar in 1 pt. of water for 2 minutes and when cool add to the must. Introduce the yeast starter and ferment for 7 days. Strain out the solids. Boil the rest of the sugar in the rest of the water and when cool add to the must. Ferment for 10 days, siphon into a 1 gal. glass bottle, and fit with a fermentation lock.

Root Wines

Many of our root vegetables make excellent wines. However, we depart from the usual procedures and cook them. They do not grow wild so you will have to buy or grow them. The soil and climate here in the mountains are both suitable for growing root crops. All the old homesteads and log cabins had either a cave or a root cellar where they stored them for winter use. Parsnips were allowed to stay in the ground, as freezing does not harm them but only makes them sweeter. Root vegetables can be used singly or in combination with other roots and grains. The following recipes are only a sampling of the many ways to make root wines.

BEET

Beets make a good wine and can be combined with other roots to make mixed root wines. Young medium-sized beets that have been freshly pulled are best for winemaking. Besides the red beet there is now an orange-colored beet that makes a light-colored wine. I have grown them in the garden but as yet have not seen them in the market.

RED BEET WINE

4 lbs. beets	1 tbs. strong tea
4 lbs. sugar	4 qts. water
2 oranges	Orange A.P. Y.S.
2 lemons	

Peel the beets and grate them into an enamel pan, being careful to catch all the juice. Add 3 qts. of water, bring to a boil, and simmer for 10 minutes. Put one-half of the sugar in a fermenting vessel and strain the beet juice over it; stir until the sugar is dissolved; discard the pulp. Dip the oranges and lemons into boiling water for a few seconds and with a sharp knife cut off a thin slice of the peel, being careful not to cut off any of the white pith. Twist the peel, to release the oil, and drop it into the must. Cut away all the white pith and discard it along with the seeds. Slice the rest of the oranges and lemons into the must. Allow the must to cool to lukewarm and introduce the yeast starter. Ferment for 7 days, stirring once each day. Strain out the solids and wring dry. Boil the rest of the sugar in the rest of the water for 2 minutes and when cool add to the must. Add the tea and allow to ferment for 10 days, siphon into a 1 gal. glass bottle, and fit with a fermentation lock.

BEET CARROT WINE

3 lbs. beets	1 tsp. Y.N.
2 lbs. carrots	1/4 tsp. tannin
3 lbs. sugar	4 qts. water
2 lemons	Orange A.P. Y.S.
2 oranges	

Scrub the carrots well and peel the beets. Grate them both into an enamel pan with 3 qts. of water. Bring to a boil, simmer for 10 minutes, removing all the scum that rises to the top. Put one-half of the sugar in a fermenting vessel and strain the liquid over it, stirring until the sugar is dissolved, and discard the pulp. Follow the same procedure as for Beet Wine.

CARROT WINE

5 lbs. carrots	2 lemons
3 lbs. sugar	2 oranges
4 oz. raisins	1 tsp. Y.N.
1-12-oz. package shredded wheat	4 qts. water
	Orange A.P. Y.S.

Scrub the carrots, grate them into an enamel pan, and add 3 qts. of water. Simmer for 20 minutes, removing all the scum. Place the chopped raisins, shredded wheat, and one-half of the sugar in a fermenting vessel. Strain the liquid over it, discard the pulp, and stir the sugar until it is dissolved. Proceed as for Beet Wine.

CARROT PARSNIP WINE

4 lbs. carrots	4 oz. chopped raisins
2 lbs. parsnips	1 tsp. Y.N.
3 lbs. sugar	4 qts. water
2 lemons	Orange A.P. Y.S.
2 oranges	

Scrub the carrots and parsnips, and cut them into thin slices into an enamel pan. Add 3 qts. of water, bring to a boil, and simmer for 15 minutes, skimming off all the scum. Be careful that the parsnips do not become too mushy. Place the chopped raisins and one-half of the sugar in a fermenting vessel, strain the liquid over them, and discard the pulp. When cool add the Y.N. and proceed as for Beet Wine.

PARSNIP WINE

4 lbs. parsnips	2 oranges
3 lbs. sugar	1 tsp. Y.N.
4 oz. chopped raisins	4 qts. water
2 lemons	Orange A.P. Y.S.

Scrub the parsnips but do not peel. Slice them into an enamel pan and add 3 qts. of water. Bring to a boil and simmer for 10 minutes, removing all the scum. Place the chopped raisins and one-half of the sugar in a fermenting vessel. Strain the liquid over them and discard the pulp. Stir until the sugar is dissolved. When cool add the Y.N. and proceed as for Beet Wine.

POTATO

After America was discovered and the potato became a staple food, it did not take long for someone to find out that potatoes also made a good wine. After they were introduced into Russia they were distilled to make vodka. Now most of the alcohol in vodka is made from petroleum by-products.

Old potatoes make the best wine — the older the better. That is the reason the mountain people always made their potato wine in the spring when the last of the potatoes were brought out of storage. Make your potato wine in the late spring when the last of the Maine potatoes reach the market.

POTATO WINE

3 lbs. old potatoes
4 lbs. sugar
4 oz. chopped raisins
2 lemons

2 oranges
1 tsp. Y.N.
5 qts. water
Orange A.P. Y.S.

Scrub the potatoes and cut out any decayed parts, but do not peel. Grate them into an enamel pan, add 3 qts. of water, bring to a boil, and simmer, removing all the scum that comes to the surface. Simmer until no more scum rises (about 15 minutes). Put 2 lbs. of the sugar and the chopped raisins into a fermenting vessel, strain the potato water over it, and stir until the sugar is dissolved. When cool add the Y.N. and proceed as for Beet Wine.

POTATO BEET WINE

4 lbs. old potatoes
1 lb. beets

4 oz. chopped raisins
1 tsp. Y.N.

3 lbs. sugar   4 qts. water
2 lemons   Orange A.P. Y.S.
2 oranges

Scrub the potatoes, removing all the decayed parts, but do not peel. Peel the beets. Grate them both into an enamel pan, add 3 qts. of water, bring to a boil, and simmer for 20 minutes, removing all the scum that rises to the top. Put one-half of the sugar and the chopped raisins in a fermenting vessel, strain the potato-beet water over them, and discard the pulp. When cool add the Y.N. and proceed as for Beet Wine.

POTATO CARROT WINE

3 lbs. old potatoes   4 oz. chopped raisins
2 lbs. carrots   4 oz. cracked wheat
3 lbs. sugar   1 tsp. Y.N.
2 lemons   5 qts. water
1 orange   Orange A.P. Y.S.

Prepare the potatoes as for Potato Wine and the carrots as for Carrot Wine. Grate them into an enamel pan, add 3 qts. of water, bring to a boil, and simmer, removing all the scum that rises to the top. Simmer until no more scum rises (10 minutes or longer). Put one-half of the sugar in a fermenting vessel and strain the potato-carrot water over it, stirring until the sugar is dissolved. Put the cracked wheat and raisins in the pan, pour 1 pt. of boiling water over them and simmer for 2 minutes; then add to the must. Allow to cool, add the Y.N., and proceed as for Beet Wine.

POTATO PARSNIP WINE

3 lbs. old potatoes	4 oz. cracked wheat
2 lbs. parsnips	1 tsp. Y.N.
3 lbs. sugar	4 qts. water
2 lemons	Orange A.P. Y.S.
1 orange	

Prepare the potatoes as for Potato Wine and the parsnips as for Parsnip Wine. Combine them and put into an enamel pan, add 3 qts. of water, bring to a boil, and simmer, removing all the scum. Simmer until no more scum rises (about 10 minutes). Put one-half of the sugar in a fermenting vessel and strain the potato-parsnip liquid over it, stirring until the sugar is dissolved. Proceed as for Potato Wine.

AN OLD-TIME RECIPE

The next recipe is an old-time favorite of the mountain people of bygone times. Each family had its own recipe and they traded back and forth. However, each winemaker had a secret ingredient he added when he made his own wine and purposely forgot to mention when he gave the recipe to someone else. One might add wheat, another corn, or still another might add a few dried apples or elder flowers. The wines were all alike, except for a fleeting taste or aroma that always eluded the drinker's identification.

Many of the homes being built today have a room called the family room, recreation room, or the Florida room. Many of the homes built in the nineteenth and early twentieth centuries had a parlor, a room shut off from the rest of the house and used or opened only for special occasions: when the preacher came to call for dinner, funerals, weddings, and if there were daughters in the family, to entertain their beaus.

Party Wine or Company Wine, too, was reserved for special events, and sometimes a jug or two would find its way to a square dance. A few jugs of this wine would liven up any party.

If you follow the directions your wine should test at around 20 percent alcohol. It is a sherry-type wine and ages well.

SMOKY MOUNTAIN PARTY WINE

10 lbs. old potatoes

15 lbs. sugar

10 oranges

5 lemons

2 lbs. raisins

2 lbs. cracked wheat

1 pkt. A.B.

1 pkt. Y.N.

5 gals. water

Orange A.P. Y.S.

Prepare the potatoes as for Potato Wine. Put 5 lbs. of the sugar in a fermenting vessel. Boil the potatoes 3 lbs. at a time, skimming off all the scum until none rises to the surface. Strain the liquid over the sugar, discard the pulp, and stir until the sugar is dissolved. Prepare the oranges and lemons as for Beet Wine. If you use whole-grain wheat, first put it in an enamel pan with the raisins and pour enough boiling water over them to cover and let simmer for 2 minutes, pour the water off and discard. Put the wheat and raisins into a blender a few at a time and chop them up coarsely. Add to the must. When the must is cool add the A.B., Y.N., and introduce the Y.S. Ferment for 7 days, stirring once each day. Boil 5 lbs. of the sugar in 1 gal. of water for 2 minutes and when cool add to the must. Ferment for 5 days but do not stir. Strain out the solids, leaving behind as much of the sediment as possible. Boil the rest of the sugar for 2 minutes in 1 gal. of water and when cool add to the must. Ferment for 10 days, siphon into a 5 gal. cubitainer or glass bottles, and fit with fermentation locks. After the last addition of sugar, if the vessel is short of 5 gallons add enough boiled and cooled water to make the 5 gallons.

If you buy all the materials for this wine, the bottled wine will cost approximately 32 cents per quart at today's prices. However, with the present creeping inflation, it will no doubt cost more by the time you read this book.

This is a smooth, semisweet, velvety type wine and resembles a good sherry. Sherry gets its burnt flavor by being aged in barrels that stand in the sun or around a furnace. You might try this with a few bottles of this wine.

SEVEN

Flower Wines

The mountain people love flowers, as a drive through the mountains, especially on any of the country roads, will reveal. The area has a wide range of native flowers, from the tiny wood violet to giant flowering trees.

The early settlers brought with them their own favorite flowering plants, and many of these have escaped and gone native or wild. The sweetbriar rose and the day lily are two good examples. In places great patches of these two plants can be seen growing without any care. Nearly every mountain cabin will have potted plants on the porch and in the yard. Regular flower pots are hard to come by so they use whatever is available — short pieces of hollow logs, old iron cooking pots, and old milk cans. The oddest one I remember seeing was a big geranium growing in a toilet bowl.

The two most widely used flowers for winemaking are the dandelion and the elderberry, but there are many more that can be used to make excellent wines. Many of these flower wines have an intriguing taste that tantalizes the taste buds.

The blossoms for flower wines should be gathered on a sunny

day as early in the day as possible after the dew has dried. Some flower wines use the whole flower; others use only the petals.

DANDELION

To many home owners the dandelion is a weed pest that gets into their lawns. However, it is a very useful plant. The leaves make good greens and are high in many of the essential vitamins. The roots when dried and roasted make a good substitute for coffee.

Dandelion blossoms appear in the spring as soon as the frost is out of the ground. So, if your lawn shows up full of the little yellow flowers this next spring don't reach for the weed-killer. Grab a basket and gather them for a delightful light table wine. Only the petals should be used. The stems are bitter, so care must be taken to avoid getting any of the stems or parts of stems in the wine mixture.

DANDELION BLOSSOM WINE

1 gal. blossoms	1 tsp. Y.N.
3 lbs. sugar	9 pts. water
2 lemons	Orange A.P. Y.S.

Pull out the petals and discard the base of the flower. Put the petals in an enamel pan with 3 qts. of water, bring to a boil, and remove from the heat. Put one-half of the sugar in a fermenting vessel, pour the contents of the pan over it, and stir until the sugar is dissolved. Allow to cool, add the juice of the lemons and the yeast nutrient. Add the Y.S. and ferment for 5 days. Strain out the solids. Boil the rest of the sugar in the rest of the water for 2 minutes and when cool add to the must. Ferment for 10 days, siphon into a 1 gallon glass bottle, and fit with a fermentation lock.

DAY LILY

Great patches of day lilies can be found growing wild here in the mountains. The flower buds, gathered just before they open, can be dipped in a batter and sautéed. They have a taste reminiscent of oysters. For winemaking the flowers should be gathered early in the morning. Be sure to shake the flowers to dislodge any insects that may be in the flower. They make a beautiful light red wine.

DAY LILY BLOSSOM WINE

1 gal. blossoms	1 tsp. Y.N.
3 lbs. sugar	9 pts. water
4 oz. chopped raisins	Orange A.P. Y.S.
1 tsp. A.B.	

Place the blossoms in an enamel pan with 7 pts. of water, bring to a boil, and remove from the heat. Cover tightly and let stand for 24 hours, stirring several times. Strain into a fermenting vessel and discard the pulp. Add the chopped raisins, A.B., and Y.N. Boil one-half of the sugar in 1 pt. of water for 2 minutes and when cool add to the must. Introduce the Y.S., and ferment for 5 days. Strain out the solids. Boil the rest of the sugar in the rest of the water for 2 minutes and when cool add to the must. Ferment for 10 days, siphon into a 1 gal. glass bottle, and fit with a fermentation lock.

ELDERBERRY

The elderberry grows in patches and is easy to spot when it is in bloom. The blossoms should be gathered in places away from highways where they are not contaminated with auto fumes and dust. The flowers should be shelled from the stems. Be careful to discard the stems.

ELDERBERRY BLOSSOM WINE

1 qt. elderberry blossoms	1 tsp. Y.N.
3 lbs. sugar	9 pts. water
8 oz. raisins	Orange A.P. Y.S.
Juice of 2 lemons	

Put the flowers in a fermenting vessel. Boil 1 lb. of sugar in 7 pts. of water for 2 minutes and pour over the flowers; cover and let stand until cool. Add the lemon juice, Y.N., and introduce the Y.S. Ferment for 5 days and then strain out the solids and discard. Boil the rest of the sugar in the rest of the water for 2 minutes and when cool add to the must. Add the chopped raisins and ferment for 10 days. Strain out the solids and allow to ferment for 5 days, siphon into a 1 gal. glass bottle, and fit with a fermentation lock.

CLOVER

White clover is another lawn flower that can be utilized to make a good table wine. We are familiar with white clover honey. Any blossom that secretes nectar for a good honey will make a good wine. Although the honey bee is unable to reach the nectar in the red clover, it still makes a good wine.

WHITE CLOVER WINE

1 gal. clover heads	1 tsp. Y.N.
3 lbs. sugar	9 pts. water

Juice of 2 lemons   Orange A.P. Y.S.

Pinch off all the stem and discard. Use only the flower heads.
Proceed as for Dandelion Wine.

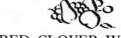

RED CLOVER WINE

1 gal. clover heads   1 tsp. Y.N.
8 oz. white raisins   9 pts. water
3 lbs. sugar   Orange A.P. Y.S.
1 tsp. A.B.

Pinch off the base, leaving only the flower heads and put them
into a fermenting vessel. Boil one-half of the sugar in 7 pts. of
water for 2 minutes and pour over the clover; cover and allow to
cool. Add the A.B., Y.N., and introduce the Y.S. Ferment for 5
days and then strain out the solids. Boil the rest of the sugar in the
rest of the water for 2 minutes and when cool add to the must. Add
the chopped raisins and ferment for 7 days. Strain out the solids
and ferment for 5 days. Siphon into a 1 gal. glass bottle and fit with
a fermentation lock.

SOURWOOD

The sourwood tree is listed in nursery catalogs as the lily of the
valley tree. The blossoms look like the tiny flowers of the lily of the
valley plant. They hang down on the stem and the bees have to
crawl upside down to get the nectar. The trees, small to medium in
size, can be seen scattered throughout the woods at blossom time,
usually during July.

SOURWOOD BLOSSOM WINE

2 qts. blossoms	1 tsp. Y.N.
3 lbs. sugar	1/4 tsp. tannin
Juice of 2 lemons	4 qts. water
1 tsp. A.B.	Orange A.P. Y.S.

Shell the blossoms from the stems and put them into a fermenting vessel. Boil 3 qts. of water, pour it over the blossoms, and allow to cool. Add the lemon juice, A.B., Y.N., and tannin. Boil one-half of the sugar in 1 pt. of water for 2 minutes and when cool add to the must. Introduce the Y.S. and ferment for 5 days. Strain out the solids. Boil the rest of the sugar in 1 pt. of water for 2 minutes and when cool add to the must. Ferment for 10 days, siphon into a 1 gal. glass bottle, and fit with a fermentation lock.

ROSE PETAL

There are many flowers suitable for winemaking and the rose ranks at the top. The people in the British Isles have been making flower wines for centuries. When they migrated to America and settled in the mountains they brought recipes for flower wines with them. The home winemaker should have a few bottles of this excellent wine in his collection to bring out on very special occasions or for just plain enjoyment.

Rose petal wines can be made with one variety and color or they can be mixed in any combination. If possible, petals from a few scented roses should be included to give the wine an aroma. The recipe that follows uses the petals of the small wild rose that grows here in the mountains. I include a handful of bright red, scented rose petals to give the wine color and aroma. It is not only one of the best wines, it is also very easy to make.

ROSE PETAL WINE

1 gal. rose petals

3 lbs. sugar

2 lemons

1 tsp. Y.N.

4 qts. water

Orange A.P. Y.S.

Put the rose petals in an enamel pan with 3 qts. of water and bring to a boil. Add one-half of the sugar, stir until the sugar is dissolved, and remove from the heat. Pour into a fermenting vessel and allow to cool. Add the Y.N. Dip the lemons in boiling water. With a sharp knife cut off a thin slice of the peel, give it a twist, and drop it into the must. Cut away all the white pith and discard it along with the seeds. Slice the rest of the lemon into the must. Introduce the Y.S. and ferment for 5 days. Strain out the solids, wringing as dry as possible. Boil the rest of the sugar in the rest of the water for 2 minutes and when cool add to the must. Ferment for 10 days, siphon into a 1 gal. glass bottle, and fit with a fermentation lock.

EIGHT

Mixed Wines

In this chapter the winemaker can let his imagination run riot. After the amateur winemaker has mastered the rudiments of winemaking he is ready to use his skill to mix them up — and anything goes. Many good wines can be the result. It is wise to keep an accurate record of all the ingredients, so that if you accidentally make a superior wine you can then duplicate the same wine in larger quantities. The possibilities are unlimited, the only restriction is the winemaker's imagination. Here are a few recipes to start you on your way to having fun with those mixed-up wines.

APPLE WHISKEY

This wine was usually made in the fall when the apples started to ripen and fall and the sweet corn became too hard to use as fresh corn. The two combine to make a very strong wine, light in color, with the aroma of sweet cider.

63

1 gal. apple juice	1 tsp. A.B.
6 ears sweet corn	1 tsp. Y.N.
2 lbs. sugar	1 pt. water
8 oz. chopped raisins	Juice A.P. Y.S.

Put the apple juice in an enamel pan. Cut and scrape the corn off the cobs and add to the apple juice. Bring to a boil and simmer for 10 minutes, skimming off all the scum that rises to the top. Add the chopped raisins and one-half of the sugar during the last two minutes of cooking. Pour into a fermenting vessel and allow to cool. Add the A.B., Y.N., and the yeast starter and ferment for 7 days, stirring once each day. Strain out the solids. Boil the rest of the sugar in 1 pt. of water for 2 minutes and when cool add to the must. Ferment for 10 days, siphon into a 1 gal. glass bottle, and fit with a fermentation lock.

APPLE BRANDY

3 qts. apple juice	1 tsp. Y.N.
2 lbs. wheat	1 qt. water
1 lb. white grapes	Juice A.P. Y.S.
3 lbs. sugar	

Put the apple juice in a fermenting vessel, add the crushed grapes, Y.N., and 1 camden tablet. Let stand for 24 hours, stirring two or three times. Boil one-half of the sugar in 1 pt. of water for 2 minutes and when cool add to the must. Introduce the Y.S. and ferment for 5 days, stirring once each day. Strain out the solids. If you use whole wheat, put it in an enamel pan, cover with boiling water, and boil for 2 minutes. Pour the water off and discard. Put the wheat in a blender, chop it coarsely, and add to the must. Boil the rest of the sugar in 1 pt. of water for 2 minutes and when cool add to the must. Ferment for 10 days, siphon into a 1 gal. glass bottle, and fit with a fermentation lock.

Note: The wheat will settle to the bottom along with the other sediments. If you use shredded wheat do not boil first.

When all fermentation has ceased and wine is ready to bottle put 1 or 2 oz. of brandy in each bottle and fill with the wine.

BLACKBERRY RAISIN WINE

5 lbs. blackberries	1 tsp. Y.N.
2 lbs. raisins	4 qts. water
Juice of 2 lemons	Juice A.P. Y.S.
3 lbs. sugar	

Put the berries in a fermenting vessel and crush them. Add the lemon juice, Y.N., 3 qts. of water, and 1 camden tablet. Let stand for 24 hours, stirring two or three times. Boil one-half of the sugar in 1 pt. of water for 2 minutes and when cool add to the must. Introduce the Y.S. and ferment for 2 days, stirring 2 times each day. Strain out the solids. Add the chopped raisins and ferment for 7 days. Strain out the solids. Boil the rest of the sugar in 1 pt. of water for 2 minutes and when cool add to the must. Ferment for 7 days, siphon into a 1 gal. glass bottle, and fit with a fermentation lock.

BLACKBERRY RHUBARB WINE

5 lbs. blackberries	1/4 tsp. tannin
2 lbs. young rhubarb	3 qts. water
3-1/2 lbs. sugar	Juice A.P. Y.S.
1 tsp. Y.N.	

Cut the rhubarb into thin slices, cover it with boiling water, and then pour the water off and away. Put the berries and rhubarb into a fermenting vessel and crush them, add Y.N., tannin, 2 qts. of water, and 1 camden tablet. Let stand for 24 hours, stirring two or three times. Boil 1-1/2 lbs. of the sugar in 1 pt. of water for 2 minutes and when cool add to the must. Introduce the Y.S. and ferment for 2 days. Strain out the solids. Add the chopped raisins. Boil the rest of the sugar in 1 pt. of water for 2 minutes and when cool add to the must. Ferment for 7 days and strain out the solids. Ferment for 5 days, siphon into a 1 gal. glass bottle, and fit with a fermentation lock.

LIGHT DRY PEAPOD ELDER FLOWER WINE

This combination may sound odd, however, it will make a good light dry table wine.

1 gal. fresh peapods	1 tsp. A.B.
1 pt. elder flowers	1 tsp. Y.N.
3 lbs. sugar	5 qts. water
4 oz. chopped raisins	Orange A.P. Y.S.

Use a pair of scissors to snip off the ends of the peapods. Put the pods into an enamel pan with the water and simmer for 30 minutes. Stir the pods several times and mash them against the side of the pan to release all the goodness in the pods. Put the sugar, chopped raisins, and elderberry flowers in a fermenting vessel and strain the boiling liquid from the pods over them. Discard the pods. Stir the liquid until the sugar is dissolved and allow to cool. Add the A.B., Y.N., and introduce the Y.S. Ferment for 7 days and then strain out the solids. Ferment for 5 days, siphon into a 1 gal. glass bottle, and fit with a fermentation lock.

TONIC WINES

This book would not be complete without mentioning tonic wines. The early mountain people, many isolated with only oxcart roads, and more than a week's travel to the nearest store and doctor, had to depend on their own skill and resources. They made most of their own tools and medicines.

In the spring, before the sap started to rise, they dug sassafras roots and peeled off the bark to make sassafras tea. They drank this to "thin the blood" after a winter of consuming such food as wild game, cured meat, canned and dried fruits and vegetables, corn meal mush, and lye hominy. One of the first things to start growing in their gardens in the spring was rhubarb, or pieplant as the mountain people called it.

Soon after the frost was out of the ground the young stalks of the rhubarb plants appeared in their gardens. They used this in a sauce as an internal cleanser. Many combined the rhubarb with herbs as in the following wine recipe.

Mountain people used many more herbs and roots as tonic plants besides the ones mentioned above — maidenhair fern root, fairywand, spotted wintergreen, Joe-pye weed, white ash bark, prickly ash bark, and so forth.

RHUBARB MINT WINE

5 lbs. young rhubarb
1 qt. mint leaves
4 lbs. sugar
1 tsp. Y.N.

1 grape leaf, chopped
4 qts. water
Orange A.P. Y.S.

Slice the rhubarb into 1/4-inch slices, cover with boiling water, and immediately pour it off and away. Put the rhubarb, mint leaves, and grape leaf in an enamel pan. Pour 3 qts. of boiling water over them and simmer for 5 minutes. Add 2 lbs. of sugar and simmer for 2 more minutes. Pour the contents into a fermenting vessel and allow to cool. Add the Y.N., introduce the Y.S., and ferment for 3 days. Strain out the solids and ferment for 5 days. Boil the rest of the sugar in the rest of the water for 2 minutes and when cool add to the must. Ferment for 5 days, siphon into a 1 gal. glass bottle, and fit with a fermentation lock.

RHUBARB SASSAFRAS WINE

5 lbs. young rhubarb
1 qt. sassafras tea
3 lbs. sugar
Juice of 2 lemons

1 tsp. Y.N.
3 qts. water
Orange A.P. Y.S.

Put one-half cup sassafras bark in an enamel pan and add 1 qt. of boiling water. Let steep for 1 hour. Slice the rhubarb into 1/4-inch slices, cover with boiling water, and immediately pour it off and away. Put the rhubarb in a fermenting vessel and crush it slightly. Boil one-half of the sugar in 2 qts. of water for 2 minutes and pour over the rhubarb. Strain the sassafras tea into the fermenting vessel and discard the bark. Allow to cool. Add the lemon juice, Y.N., and introduce the Y.S. Ferment for 2 days and then strain out the solids. Ferment for 5 days. Boil the rest of the sugar in 1 qt. of water and when cool add to the must. Ferment for 10 days, siphon into a 1 gal. glass bottle, and fit with a fermentation lock.

NINE

Honey Wines

Fermented honey, called mead, was probably man's first wine. Very little mead is made today because honey is much more expensive than sugar and requires a longer aging period. Mead made in quantity and aged in wood casks can take up to 9 years to mature.

Mead is mentioned in the old Norse and Greek legends. It was used in ancient religious ceremonies and was supposed to have supernatural healing powers. It was also thought to be a restorer of manly vigor.

Honey wine is said to be one of the gifts that the Queen of Sheba took with her when she visited King Solomon. She presented the wine in urns of gold as a "gift of the gods." Is it any wonder that she received such a royal welcome in the courts of King Solomon.

The Greeks called the wine hydromel, which means honey and water. Later fruit juice was added; it was then called melomel. Later, when herbs and spices were added by the Romans and Welsh, it became known as metheglin.

The early mountain people were poor as far as money was

concerned and had to use sugar sparingly. However most kept bees, and when there was a favorable honey season they had a surplus.

They kept their bees in "bee-gums," sections of hollow logs, usually from the blackgum tree, and put a box or crock on top of the gum where the bees stored the surplus honey. They were superstitious and many legends grew up around their way of living and their bees. One such legend was that they never counted their bee-gums, for it would bring bad luck. If a stranger was to ask one of the mountain men how many bee-gums he had, the answer would be, "Well I don't rightly know how many there be." Another superstition stated that if there was a death in the family it was the duty of the next of kin to go tell the bees; otherwise, the bees would all die.

It was only natural that the mountain people learned to use honey in the place of sugar in making their homemade wines. However, both honey and fruit contain many wild yeasts and bacteria, especially bacteria which produce vinegar. The only method available to them was to boil the honey and fruit juice before fermenting it into wine to kill the vinegar bacteria. That is the reason that most of the old-time recipes called for boiling the honey and juice before fermenting.

In the fall when the apples glowed red and golden in the afternoon sun and the old mill filled the air with the aroma of sweet cider as the juice flowed from the press, it was time to make apple honey wine. A more delightful wine is hard to find.

APPLEJACK HONEY WINE

1 gal. apple cider	1 tsp. A.B.
3 lbs. mountain honey	1 tsp. Y.N.
4 oz. chopped raisins	Juice mead or A.P. Y.S.

Put the cider and honey in an enamel pan and bring to a boil. Simmer for 15 minutes, skimming off all the scum that rises to the surface. After 10 minutes add the chopped raisins. Remove from the heat, cover, and allow to cool. Pour into a fermenting vessel, add the A.B., Y.N., and introduce the yeast starter. Ferment for 5 days and then strain out the solids. Allow to ferment for 10 days, siphon into a 1 gal. glass bottle, and fit with a fermentation lock.

Note: It takes honey wines longer to finish fermentation, so do not be in a hurry to bottle. Honey wines should be aged one year or longer to reach their maximum goodness.

GRAPES

All types of grapes, wild and domestic, can be used to make honey wines. You can also buy grape concentrate from wine supply stores. The following recipe calls for the blue concord usually found in the stores in early fall.

GRAPE HONEY WINE

5 lbs. concord grapes	3 qts. water
3 lbs. light honey	Juice A.P. Y.S.

Put the grapes in a fermenting vessel and crush them. Add the honey and enough boiled and cooled water to make 1 gal. Add 1 camden tablet and let stand for 24 hours, stirring two or three times. Introduce the Y.S. and ferment for 5 days. Strain out the solids. Ferment for 10 days, siphon into a 1 gal. glass bottle, and fit with fermentation lock. When all fermentation has ceased, add 1 camden tablet and let stand for 24 hours before bottling for storing.

PEACHES, APRICOTS, AND NECTARINES

All three of these fruits make good honey wines. They are made similarly; the one here is for peaches. A few rhubarb stalks added to these fruit honey wines help bring out the aroma and flavor.

PEACH RHUBARB HONEY WINE

5 lbs. peaches	1/4 tsp. tannin
1 lb. young rhubarb	7 pts. water
3 lbs. honey	Orange A.P. Y.S.
1 tsp. Y.N.	

If you use cultivated peaches it is best to remove the peel, for they have been sprayed with both insecticides and fungicides. The small wild mountain peach does not need to be peeled. Prepare the peaches and slice into a fermenting vessel. You can either discard the pits or toss them into the fermenting vessel. (They will add flavor and color to the wine.) Slice the rhubarb into 1/4-inch slices. Pour boiling water to cover over the rhubarb and immediately pour the water off and away. Add the rhubarb to the peaches. Add the honey, Y.N., tannin, and enough boiled and cooled water to make 1 gallon. Add 2 camden tablets and allow to stand for 24 hours, stirring two or three times. Introduce the Y.S. and ferment for 2 days after fermentation starts. Strain out the solids and allow to ferment for 10 days. Siphon into a 1 gal. glass bottle and fit with a fermentation lock.

BERRIES AND EXOTIC FRUITS

Light colored berries make good honey wines. Sweet cherries and red plums are also excellent. If you want a really exotic wine there is the Chinese lichee fruit. The fresh fruit is seldom available, but you can find the canned variety in most large markets. Cultivated berries as well as the wild kind can be used.

WILD RASPBERRY HONEY WINE

4 lbs. raspberries	1 tsp. A.B.
4 oz. chopped raisins	3 qts. water
2 lbs. orange blossom honey	Orange A.P. Y.S.
1 tsp. Y.N.	

Put the berries in a fermenting vessel and crush them. Add the honey, Y.N., A.B., and enough boiled and cooled water to make 1 gal. Add 2 camden tablets and let stand for 24 hours, stirring two or three times. Introduce the Y.S. and ferment for 3 days. Strain out the solids, add the chopped raisins, and ferment for 10 days. Siphon into a 1 gal. glass bottle and fit with a fermentation lock.

STRAWBERY HONEY WINE

4 lbs. strawberries	1 tsp. Y.N.
2 lbs. clover honey	7 pts. water
4 oz. chopped raisins	Orange A.P. Y.S.
1 tsp. A.B.	

Follow the same method as for raspberry wine.

CITRUS HONEY WINES

Many of the citrus fruits can be combined with honey to make good wines. The best are orange, tangerine, calamondin, and the Key lime. The Key lime was so named because it was grown on the

Florida Keys to supply the British Navy with citrus juice, during the sailing ship era, as a scurvy preventative.

ORANGE HONEY WINE

6 large navel oranges   1/4 tsp. tannin
4 lbs. orange blossom honey   Water to 1 gal.
1 tsp. malic acid   Orange A.P. Y.S.
1 tsp. Y.N.

Drop the oranges into boiling water for a few seconds and then throw the water away. With a sharp knife remove a thin slice of the peel, being careful not to cut off any of the white pith. Twist the peel to release the oils, and drop it into a fermenting vessel. Cut off all the white pith and discard it along with the seeds. Slice the rest of the orange into the fermenting vessel. Add the honey, M.A., Y.N., tannin, enough boiled and cooled water to make 1 gal., and 1 camden tablet. Let stand for 24 hours, stirring two or three times. Introduce the Y.S. and ferment for 5 days. Strain out the solids, wringing out as much of the liquid as possible. Ferment for 10 days, siphon into a 1 gal. glass bottle, and fit with a fermentation lock. When fermentation ceases add 1 camden tablet and let stand 24 hours before bottling.

KUMQUAT HONEY WINE

1 qt. fully ripe kumquats   1/4 tsp. tannin
3 lbs. orange blossom honey   Water to 1 gal.
1 tsp. malic acid   Orange A.P. Y.S.
1 tsp. Y.N.

Wash the fruit in running water. Slice the whole fruit into a fermenting vessel and proceed as for Orange Honey Wine.

TANGERINE HONEY WINE

12 ripe tangerines	1/4 tsp. tannin
4 lbs. orange blossom honey	Water to 1 gal.
1 tsp. malic acid	Orange A.P. Y.S.
1 tsp. Y.N.	

Wash the tangerines in running water and slice the whole fruit into a fermenting vessel. Proceed as for Orange Honey Wine.

HONEY FLOWER WINES

Many blossoms can be utilized to make excellent honey wines. The blossoms should be picked on a dry day in places where there are no dust or car emissions. Blossoms cannot be washed without losing the flavor and aroma which the winemaker is trying to catch in his honey wines.

CLOVER BLOSSOM HONEY WINE

1 gal. clover blossoms, white or red	1 tsp. A.B.
	1 tsp. Y.N.
2 lbs. clover honey	Water to 1 gal.
1 lb. sugar	Orange A.P. Y.S.
4 oz. white raisins	

Place the blossoms in a fermenting vessel and pour 3 qts. of boiling water over them. Cool. Add the honey, A.B., Y.N., and 1 camden tablet. Let stand for 24 hours, stirring two or three times. Ferment for 5 days and then strain out the solids. Boil the sugar and chopped raisins in 1 qt. of water for 2 minutes and when cool add to the must. Ferment for 7 days and then strain out the solids. Ferment for 5 days, siphon into a 1 gal. glass bottle, and fit with a fermentation lock.

DANDELION BLOSSOM HONEY WINE

1 gal. dandelion flowers	1 tsp. A.B.
2 lbs. honey	1 tsp. Y.N.
1 lb. sugar	4 qts. water
4 oz. raisins	Orange A.P. Y.S.

Pull out the petals and discard the base and all stems, which are very bitter. Follow the method used for Clover Blossom Wine.

SOURWOOD BLOSSOM HONEY WINE

1 qt. sourwood blossoms	1/4 tsp. tannin
3 lbs. honey	4 qts. water
1 tsp. A.B.	Orange A.P. Y.S.
1 tsp. Y.N.	

Use sourwood honey if available, or any good table honey. Place the flowers and honey in a fermenting vessel and pour 4 qts. of boiling water over them. Stir until the honey is dissolved. Add the A.B., Y.N., and 1 camden tablet. Let stand for 24 hours, stirring two or three times. Introduce the Y.S. and ferment for 7 days. Strain out the solids, ferment for 10 days, siphon into a 1 gal. glass bottle, and fit with a fermentation lock.

TEN

Grain Wines

The mountain people are noted for their "corn squeezins'," but that is another story and does not belong here. However, good wine can be made from grains, and this book would not be complete without a few of the best mountain recipes for grain wines.

You can feel the warming effect of this one clear to the ends of your toes.

WINTER SPECIAL WINE

2 lbs. cracked wheat
4 oz. raisins
12 peppercorns
1 tsp. instant coffee
1 tsp. A.B.

1 tsp. Y.N.
4 qts. water
Orange A.P. Y.S.
3 lbs. sugar

Rinse the wheat and raisins in cold water and put them in an enamel pan with 2 qts. of water. Bring to a boil and let boil lightly

77

for 2 minutes. Pour into a fermenting vessel. Boil one-half of the sugar in 1 qt. of water for 2 minutes and add to the must. Let stand until cool. Add the peppercorns, A.B., Y.N., and introduce the Y.S. Ferment for 10 days and then strain out the solids. Boil the rest of the sugar in 1 qt. of water and when cool add to the must. Ferment for another 10 days, siphon into a 1 gallon glass bottle, and fit with a fermentation lock.

CORN

Gone are the cornfields with their rows of corn shocks and pumpkins shining golden in the autumn sun. Gone are the corn shuckings when mountain folks got together to shuck a neighbor's corn and enjoy a harvest dinner, the married folks to talk crops and politics, the young to carry on their courtships. Gone are the days when a jug of hard cider was passed around to the harvest hands. Technology and modern harvesting machines are hurrying our civilization, but to where? If you can find a leisure moment you can still enjoy the cornshucker's wine.

CORN SHUCKIN' WINE

3 lbs. cracked corn	Juice of 2 lemons
3 lbs. sugar	1 tsp. Y.N.
1 lb. chopped raisins	4 qts. water
2 tart apples	Orange A.P. Y.S.

Put the cracked corn into an enamel pan with 3 qts. of water and bring to a boil. Keep hot, just below the boiling point, for about 45 minutes. Add 1 lb. of sugar, the apples that have been cored and chopped, and the chopped raisins. Bring to a boil, remove from the heat, and allow to cool. Pour into a fermenting vessel, add the lemon juice, Y.N., and introduce the Y.S. Ferment for 5 days. Boil 1 lb. of sugar in 1 pt. of water for 2 minutes. When cool add to the must. Ferment for 5 days and strain out the solids. Boil the rest of the sugar in the rest of the water for 2 minutes and when cool add to the must. Ferment for 5 days, siphon into a 1 gal. glass bottle, and fit with a fermentation lock.

OATS

Many of the early settlers who found their way into the mountains came from the highlands of Scotland. Oatmeal or oat porridge was one of the staples of their diet, and when they could spare a little or had a surplus they made a batch of oat wine. Even if you never had a Mac attached to your name, you can still enjoy a good oat wine to remind you of the past.

MAC'S OAT WINE

1 large box regular oatmeal	1 tsp. A.B.
4 oz. chopped raisins	1 tsp. Y.N.
3 lbs. sugar	1 tbs. tea
1 gal. water	Orange A.P. Y.S.

Dump the oatmeal into a fermenting vessel. Boil one-half of the sugar and the chopped raisins in 3 qts. of water for 2 minutes and pour over the oatmeal. Allow to cool then add the A.B., Y.N., and the tea. Ferment for 7 days and strain out the solids. Boil the rest of the sugar in 1 qt. of water for 2 minutes and when cool add to the must. Ferment for 10 days, siphon into a 1 gal. glass bottle, and fit with a fermentation lock.

RICE

The Japanese make a wine they call sake by fermenting rice. It has a high alcohol content and is served warm in Japan. It is also good very cold. The alcohol content is brought about by adding the sugar in stages. Use an all-purpose yeast and keep the must working as long as possible. It is best to use the natural brown rice which many groceries and health food stores carry today.

RICE WINE (SAKE)

1 lb. brown rice	1 tsp. A.B.
4 lbs. sugar	9 pts. water
1/4 tsp. green tea leaves	A.P. Yeast

Put the rice into an enamel pan with 3 qts. of water and allow it to soak for 12 hours or overnight. Bring the rice to a boil and simmer for 30 minutes. Add 1 lb. of sugar during the last 2 minutes of cooking. When cool pour into a fermenting vessel, add the A.B. and green tea leaves. (No other kind will do.) Sprinkle 1 pkt. of all-purpose yeast over the top and ferment for 5 days. Boil 1 lb. of sugar in 1 pt. of water for 2 minutes and when cool add to the must. Ferment for 5 days and then add another pound of sugar as above. Ferment for 5 days and carefully siphon into a 1 gal. glass bottle, leaving behind all the sediment. Boil the rest of the sugar in the rest of the water for 2 minutes and when cool fill the bottle to the top. Fit with a fermentation lock and allow the wine to finish. It should be as clear as water, with an alcohol content of from 18 to 20 percent.

ELEVEN

Tropical
and Exotic Wines

The land mass that makes up the Florida peninsula is young, compared to many other land masses of the world. When Columbus made his voyage across the Atlantic Ocean, and discovered the Americas, there were few kinds of fruits growing in South Florida. He found the seagrape, saw-palmetto berry, cocoplum, custard apple, huckleberry, and a few coconut trees growing along the shore. Most of the fruits that grow there today have been introduced from other parts of the world.

The Chinese lichee fruit, native to China, and considered by many to be one of the world's most exotic fruits, was introduced into Florida early in this century. The first planting was at Laurel, Florida. While the tree grows and thrives, its fruiting habit is rather erratic. There are a few commercial plantings, but most of the fruit is consumed locally.

The canned fruit, available in most large stores, can be used for winemaking. The following recipe calls for the fresh fruit.

LICHEE FRUIT WINE

3 lbs. lichee fruit   1/4 tsp. tannin
3 lbs. orange blossom honey   7 pts. water
1 tsp. A.B.   Champagne Y.S.
1 tsp. Y.N.

Peel and remove the seeds, being careful not to lose any of the juice. Discard the peel and seeds. Put the fruit in a fermenting vessel and add the honey, A.B., Y.N., tannin, and 6 pts. water that has been boiled and cooled. Add 1 camden tablet and let stand for 24 hours, stirring two or three times. Introduce the Y.S., ferment for 2 days, and strain out the solids. Add the rest of the water (or enough to make 1 gal.) that has been boiled and cooled. Ferment for 10 days, siphon into a 1 gal. glass bottle, and fit with a fermentation lock. Add 1 camden tablet 24 hours before the wine is to be bottled.

Note: This wine should age for at least one year in the bottles — two is better. This is a delightful wine with an exotic aroma and taste.

MANGO

The mango, to my taste, is the world's most exotic and delicious fruit. Native to India and introduced into Florida via South America, one of the original imports, the mulgoba, is the parent tree of many of the existing varieties grown there today. From a mulgoba seed came the haden, named after the man who planted it, and from haden seeds many, many more varieties, as each seed produces a fruit a little different from all the others. While the mango is related to poison ivy and poison oak, there is no poison in the fruit.

The pineapple is another fruit with an irresistible aroma that at one time grew on hundreds of acres in South Florida. Cities now stand or are being built on former pineapple fields. The two combined produce a dessert wine that is beyond comparison.

SWEET MANGO-PINEAPPLE DESSERT WINE

6 lbs. ripe mangoes	1 tsp. Y.N.
1 large pineapple	1/4 tsp. tannin
3-1/2 lbs. sugar	4 qts. water
1 tsp. A.B.	Orange A.P. Y.S.

Peel the mangoes and discard the peel. Slice into a fermenting vessel and discard the seeds. Peel the pineapple, discard the peel, and slice the rest into the fermenting vessel. Add 3 qts. of water that has been boiled and cooled. Add 1 camden tablet and let stand for 24 hours, stirring two or three times. Boil one-half of the sugar in 1 pt. of water for 2 minutes and when cool add to the must. Introduce the Y.S. Ferment for 3 days, stirring once each day, and then strain out the solids. Boil the rest of the sugar in the rest of the water for 2 minutes and when cool add to the must. Ferment for 10 days, siphon into a 1 gal. glass bottle, and fit with a fermentation lock.

ROSEAPPLE

The roseapple is another fruit from India. It is a small yellow fruit, hollow inside, with 2 or 3 large seeds. The taste and aroma are reminiscent of roses, hence the common name. The tree is well adapted to Florida. The first blooms appear in December and the fruit starts ripening in February through April.

ROSEAPPLE APERITIF WINE

5 lbs. roseapples
3 lbs. sugar
Juice of 2 lemons
Juice of 2 oranges
1 tsp. A.B.

1 tsp. Y.N.
1/4 tsp. tannin
4 qts. water
Orange A.P. Y.S.

Cut away the blossom end of the fruit and discard along with the seeds. Cut the rest of the fruit into a fermenting vessel. Boil one-half of the sugar in 3 qts. of water, pour over the fruit, and let stand until cool. Add the A.B., Y.N., and tannin. Introduce the yeast starter and ferment for 3 days, stirring once each day. Strain out the solids. Add the orange and lemon juice and ferment for 5 days. Boil the rest of the sugar in the rest of the water for 2 minutes and when cool add to the must. Ferment for 10 days, siphon into a 1 gal. glass bottle, and fit with a fermentation lock.

SURINAM CHERRY

The Surinam cherry, native to Brazil, is so common in Florida that it is sometimes called the Florida cherry. It is used by nurseries as a hedge plant. A single specimen will grow into a small tree if the root sprouts are kept pruned. The fruit is larger than the common cherry and is sweet when fully ripe. There are both red and black varieties. Either variety makes a good wine with an exotic flavor that is impossible to describe.

SURINAM CHERRY WINE

1 gal. Surinam cherries
2-1/2 lbs. sugar
Juice of 2 oranges

1 tsp. Y.N.
3 qts. water
Juice A.P. Y.S.

Remove the pits and place the rest of the fruit in a fermenting vessel. Add the orange juice, 2 qts. of water, and 1 camden tablet. Let stand for 24 hours, stirring two or three times. Boil 1-1/2 lbs. of the sugar in 1 qt. of water for 2 minutes and when cool add to the must. Introduce the yeast starter and ferment for 2 days. Strain out the pulp and allow to ferment for 5 days. Boil the rest of the sugar in the rest of the water for 2 minutes and when cool add to the must. Ferment for 10 days, siphon into a 1 gal. glass bottle, and fit with a fermentation lock.

CARAMBOLA

The carambola, a fruit from tropical Asia, was introduced into South Florida, where it found the soil and climate to its liking. The fruit is oblong with serrated ridges running lengthwise. The color is light yellow and it has the appearance of being waxed. Cut crosswise and laid flat it resembles a star. The ripe fruit can be eaten out of hand; however, until it is fully ripe it is very tart. Sliced thin, with a little honey and creme de menthe added it makes a good accompaniment for a dinner.

CARAMBOLA WINE

6 lbs. carambolas
3-1/2 lbs. sugar

1/4 tsp. tannin
7 pts. water

Juice of 2 lemons   Orange A.P. Y.S.
1 tsp. Y.N.

Slice the fruit into a fermenting vessel and add 5 pts. of water
that has been boiled and cooled. Add 1 camden tablet and let stand
for 24 hours, stirring two or three times. Boil 1-1/2 lbs. of the
sugar in 1 pt. of water for 2 minutes and when cool add to the must.
Add the Y.N. and introduce the Y.S. Ferment for 2 days and strain
out the solids. Add the lemon juice and tannin and ferment for 5
days. Boil the rest of the sugar in 1 pt. of water for 2 minutes and
when cool add to the must. Ferment for 7 days, siphon into a 1 gal.
glass bottle, and fit with a fermentation lock.

TOMATO

This is a recent experiment and I don't know where else to list it.
It turned out to be good wine. Contrary to what you might expect
it is almost clear; the red of the tomatoes settles out during
fermentation.

RED RIPE TOMATO WINE

5 lbs. ripe tomatoes   2 B. complex tablets
3 lbs. sugar   6 vitamin C tablets
1 tsp. A.B.   6 pts. water
1 tsp. Y.N.   Baker's yeast
1 tbs. tea   All-purpose yeast

Dip the tomatoes into boiling water for 1 minute, remove the
skins, cut out the ends, and slice into a fermenting vessel. Add the
A.B., Y.N., tea, B. complex, and vitamin C. Boil one-half of the

sugar in 5 pts. of water for 2 minutes and when cool add to the must. Mix the bakers' yeast to a paste in a little boiled and cooled water. Spread it on a slice of toasted bread and place the bread, yeast side down, on the must. Ferment for 5 days and strain out the solids. Boil the rest of the sugar in 1 pt. of water for 2 minutes and when cool add to the must. Sprinkle 1/4 tsp. of all-purpose yeast on top of the must and ferment for 10 days. Siphon into a 1 gal. glass bottle and fit with a fermentation lock.

TWELVE

Notes and Shortcuts

How does the cost of homemade wines compare to the cost of commercial wines? The cost depends on several factors. If you purchase all the materials, the wine will cost more than if you gather wild fruits and berries or grow them in your yard or garden.

Wine books will tell you that you can make homemade wines for as little as ten cents per gallon. However, this is rather farfetched as the minimum sugar in a gallon of wine is 2 pounds, for a cost of 25 cents at today's prices. If you will turn back to Chapter Six you will note that Smoky Mountain Party Wine, where all the material was purchased, cost approximately 32 cents per quart. The cheapest wine you can buy sells for about $1.50 per fifth, so you can see there is a substantial saving.

However, the money saved is not the only advantage in making your own wine. Many chemicals are used in the process of making commercial wines. The only chemical the home winemaker needs is camden tablets (sulfur dioxide) which is only a fruit-preserving chemical and oxidizes out as the wine is fermented.

SANITATION

Sanitation is the watchword for the home winemaker. Wild yeasts and bacteria are everywhere, in the air and on all objects. Most are friendly, but there are some, like vinegar-producing bacteria, that can ruin wine. All vessels and instruments used in winemaking must be sterile. This is now easy with the use of camden tablets. All water used should be boiled and cooled. Sugar should be added as a syrup by being boiled for 2 minutes in the amount of water to be used.

All fermenting vessels, wooden spoons, etc., should be sterilized in a camden solution and then rinsed with boiled water. Bottles for storing wine should be washed in detergent and rinsed thoroughly. To sterilize, dissolve 1 camden tablet in one-half gallon of boiled and cooled water. Pour some of this solution in a bottle and shake. Pour into the next bottle and repeat until all bottles have been sterilized. Rinse out with a little boiled and slightly cooled water. Dip the stoppers in the solution, rinse, and put on the bottles until ready to fill.

COVERS

All wine vessels should be kept tightly covered when not being worked. This is necessary as the surrounding air is full of wild yeasts and bacteria. The best cover I have found is a plastic bag sized to fit over the fermenting vessel. Buy several yards of dressmaker's elastic. Cut a length a little smaller than the vessel and sew the ends together. Slip the plastic bag over the top of the vessel and fasten with the elastic band. You now have an almost airtight cover that will exclude the outside air but will allow the gas (carbon dioxide) created by the fermentation to escape. The bag will be inflated by the gas, and you can tell at a glance when fermentation slows or stops and the wine is ready for more sugar or siphoning into bottles for polishing and finishing.

STRAINING

A double layer of cheesecloth makes a good strainer for straining out the solids from the must. Buy the better grade as it will work better and last longer. The cloth should be boiled before each use. Here is a tip that can save you time and trouble. First place a layer of cheesecloth over the vessel and fasten it with the elastic band. Put a double layer over this for the strainer. When gathering up the ends to squeeze out the pulp, if you happen to spill some, the cloth over the vessel will catch it. Except when wine contains solids that need to be removed it is best to use a siphon, which leaves all the sediment behind. The more times a wine is racked, the less sediment in the finished wine, and the clearer it will be.

BOTTLING

How do you know when a wine is ready to bottle for storing? The wine should be perfectly clear or, in wine usage, polished. All fermentation should cease. Have a strong flashlight or a spotlight handy and shine it through the bottle. There should be no haze and no bubbles rising. Most wines will clear in time so don't be in a hurry to bottle. Be sure to fill the bottles to the top so as to exclude all air. Colored bottles are best, but if you do not intend to store the wine for any length of time, clear bottles can be used.

STORAGE

Most houses, sad to relate, have no basements, attics, or other storage facilities. There is one advantage, however, in that some modern homes are air conditioned and maintain an even temperature the year around which is ideal for wine storage. Find a closet or nook where your wine is in a dark cool place (50°–55° F) and it will take care of itself and age properly. Hobbies are for fun and relaxation, so don't worry. The wine you thought was only mediocre at bottling time may, when opened, be a prize winner.

AGING

How long should wine age in the bottles or how soon can it be drunk? Wine requires time in the making and aging. Homebrew or beer can be made and drunk in a matter of days, but not so wine. After wine is siphoned into bottles for polishing and finishing it will work or ferment for two weeks to three months.

After the finished wine is bottled, it should be labeled with the date it was bottled and the approximate date that it should be opened. Dry wines made from fresh fruits or berries are ready to drink when fermentation ceases, but they will improve if left to age. They should never be opened before 6 months or a year. Flower wines need to age somewhat longer, one year being about the minimum.

The full-bodied wines, like port and burgundy, need to be aged for two years and longer to reach their maximum goodness.

Honey wines need to age one year or longer. Some types of mead, when aged in casks, need to be aged up to nine years. However, where fruit juices or flower blossoms are used, they require less time and are good after one year.

There are no set rules for aging. If you have several bottles of any variety, you can always open a bottle any time to see how it is aging.

SERVING WINE

Most homemade wines will have a little sediment in the bottom of the bottle so it is a good idea to decant the wine before chilling or serving. Using a good light, pour the wine into another bottle, being careful to leave all the sediment behind. You will lose a little wine, but you will not have to be careful when pouring it into the serving glasses.

Some prefer a sweet or semisweet wine. If you wish to sweeten a dry wine it can be done easily. Pour a little of the wine in a small enamel pan, add the desired amount of sugar, and heat until the sugar is dissolved. Pour back into the bottle and chill. A little mild honey, like orange blossom, is even better than sugar.

Wine should be served in a stemmed glass. You can find wine glasses in the marketplace for each type of wine. However, most of us settle for an all-purpose glass, which should hold 8–10 oz. and be clear. The glass should be filled about two-thirds full so that the wine can be swished around to get the full aroma.

THIRTEEN

Cooking with Wine

Wine in the kitchen should be considered as a flavoring. When used with meats it acts as a tenderizer. The meat should be browned before the wine is added, and then simmered very slowly to finish cooking. The alcohol evaporates at boiling temperature, leaving only the flavoring.

A dry wine is best for cooking meats; otherwise you will be adding some sweetness to the cooked food. The less expensive wines can be used in cooking. Your best wines should be drunk and enjoyed. The so-called cooking wines you see in the stores are a waste of your money.

If you have used wines you are no doubt familiar, or have heard, that you should use a red wine with red meat and a white wine with white meat. This was put out by the wine industry to sell more wine. You can forget about this rule. There is perhaps one exception: fish sauces are better made with a white wine.

Wine used in meat marinades acts as a tenderizer because of its acids which soften the meat tissues exposed to it through marinating or simmering. The meat, if it is to be roasted or broiled, should be thoroughly dried before cooking.

Most soups are improved with the addition of a tablespoon or more of wine. The wine should be added just before serving, a tablespoon at a time, and tasted after each addition.

It is customary in this age of affluence to serve drinks and hors d'oeuvres before dinner. Just about every food known has at some time found its way onto the hors d'oeuvres plate. Cheese in every variety and combination is often used. The following original recipe for a cheese ball has always made a big impression whenever and wherever served.

CHEESE BALL MAHAN

1 lb. process cheddar
1 lb. block cream cheese
1/2 lb. Danish blue cheese
1/4 lb. French Roquefort
1 cup pecan meal
1/4 cup minced onion, dry
1/4 cup chopped parsley
1/4 cup chopped chives
4 tbs. worcestershire sauce
1/2 cup chopped pecans
2 tbs. chopped parsley

To make pecan meal, place pecans in a blender and turn on and off several times. Remove cheese from refrigerator and allow to soften. Place all ingredients except the last two in a large mixing bowl. Use a heavy two-pronged fork, like the one from a carving set, to mix the ingredients thoroughly. Shape into a ball and wrap in oiled paper and foil. Refrigerate until the cheese is set and the flavors blended. Put the chopped pecans and parsley in the bowl and roll the cheese around to cover. Wrap and refrigerate until about an hour before serving time. To serve, place on a tray with a cheese knife and crackers on the side.

Note: When the cheese ball has set you can cut it into fourths, roll each fourth in the pecans and parsley, and then place them back together in a ball. You can then serve one fourth at a time. The rest can be frozen if intended to be kept longer than 10 days.

Caution: When handling cheese never touch the cheese with your hands. That will cause the cheese to mold.

Probably the most famous wine recipe is chicken cooked in champagne. Here is my version:

CHICKEN MADAME POMPADOUR

4 small chicken breasts with wings attached
8 small fresh pork sausage links
6 French shallots, chopped
1 small can truffles, thinly sliced
  (or a 2-oz. can of sliced mushrooms)
1 cup champagne
1/2 cup chicken broth
2 tbs. flour
2 tbs. butter
1/2 cup heavy cream
1 tsp. lemon juice
Salt and white pepper to taste

Use only the white meat of the chicken. If the breasts are large they should be cut in half, allowing one half for each serving. Cut off the first joint of the chicken wing and discard.

Salt and pepper the chicken and brown it lightly in a skillet with a little butter. Transfer to a pan with a lid or a Corning Ware® cooking dish and add the sausages, shallots, truffles, champagne, and chicken broth. Simmer gently for about 45 minutes or until the meat is tender. Remove the chicken and sausage to a heated platter or serving dish and keep warm. Mix the butter and flour into a paste and add it to the sauce bit by bit. Cook for a few minutes until the sauce thickens. Add the lemon juice and cream. Heat, but do not let it boil after adding the cream.

Spoon a little of the sauce over the chicken and sprinkle with a little chopped parsley. Serve the rest of the sauce in a gravy boat. Serve with steamed rice. Serves four.

CHICKEN LIVERS IN WINE SAUCE

1 lb. chicken livers
2 tbs. cooking oil
4 tbs. butter
1/4 cup flour
1 4-oz. cup chopped shallots or onions
1 4-oz. can sliced mushrooms or 1/4 lb. fresh
1/4 cup white or red wine
Salt and white pepper to taste

Season the flour with salt and pepper and dust over the livers. Heat a heavy skillet and add 2 tbs. of the butter and the oil. Brown the livers quickly a few at a time if pan is not large enough. Have another pan, Corning Ware® or electric frying pan, ready. Melt the rest of the butter in the second pan and add the shallots and mushrooms if fresh. Cook until the shallots are tender but not brown. As the livers brown transfer to the other pan. When all are browned pour the wine over them, cover and simmer for 10 minutes or until the desired doneness is reached. Serves four.

SWEDISH MEATBALLS (BUFFET STYLE)

The spices in these meatballs create a distinctive taste that your guests will wonder about.

3 tbs. butter
4 tbs. cooking oil
3 tbs. finely chopped onion
3/4 cup light cream
1/4 cup dry wine
3/4 cup dry bread crumbs
1-1/2 lb. ground lean beef, chuck or round
1/2 lb. ground lean pork
2 eggs slightly beaten
1 tsp. salt or to taste
1/4 tsp. pepper
1/4 tsp. allspice
1/4 tsp. ginger
pinch of cloves

SAUCE

2 tbs. flour
1/4 cup light cream
1 tsp. salt
dash of pepper
1/2 tsp. bottled gravy seasoning

Sauté the onion in 1 tbs. butter until golden. In a large mixing bowl combine the 3/4 cup cream, wine, and bread crumbs. Allow to stand until bread crumbs are soft. Add the sautéed onions, ground meat, eggs, salt, pepper, and spices. Toss lightly but thoroughly to mix. Shape into small meat balls with a teaspoon. Put the rest of the butter and the oil in the skillet in which the onions were cooked, and sauté the meatballs a few at a time, until browned on all sides. Add more oil if needed. Transfer the meatballs to a heated platter or chafing dish and keep warm. To make the sauce, stir the flour into the skillet in which the meatballs were cooked, until it is smooth. Gradually stir in one-half cup water and the cream, stirring constantly. Bring just to a boil. Add salt and pepper to taste and a little more wine if desired. Add the meatballs and heat until heated through. Garnish with parsley. Serves 6 to 8.

Note: Can be served without the sauce.

Imagine if you can a Saint Patrick's Day dinner without corned beef and cabbage. The secret in cooking corned beef is not to let it boil. It takes a lot of watching, for corned beef must cook for several hours. However, it is well worth watching to have a delicious tender corned beef. Allow 1/2 to 3/4 lb. per serving.

CORNED BEEF AND CABBAGE DINNER — SAINT PATRICK

1-4 lb. corned beef
1 bottle dry white or red wine
2 bay leaves
6 peppercorns
1 small clove garlic
1 lb. small onions
1 lb. carrots
1 medium head cabbage, cut into wedges

Most corned beef now comes in sealed packages with directions for preparation and cooking. Place the corned beef in a large kettle; cover with about 1/3 wine and water. Add the bay leaves, peppercorns, and garlic and simmer until tender (about 3 hours).

Never let it boil. When done, remove the beef to a hot platter and keep hot. Strain out the bay leaves and peppercorns. Put the remaining vegetables in the kettle and cook until tender. Serves six or eight.

Wine can also be used in vegetable cooking. Here are a few recipes from my files:

NEW POTATOES STEAMED IN WINE

8 medium new potatoes
2 tbs. chopped onions
2 tbs. butter
1/4 cup white wine
Salt and pepper to taste
1 tbs. minced parsley

Wash and scrape the potatoes. Place the potatoes, onion, and wine in a heavy saucepan, cover and simmer until potatoes are tender, adding more wine if necessary. If any wine is left in pan, remove the cover, and cook at high heat until it evaporates. Add the butter, salt, pepper, and minced parsley and stir until the potatoes are coated. Serves four.

CARROTS IN WINE

1 lb. young carrots
2 tbs. butter
1/4 cup sherry-type wine
Salt and pepper to taste

Wash and scrape the carrots clean; if much larger than a pencil, cut in half lengthwise. Sauté the carrots in the butter, turning them until they are coated. Sprinkle with salt, pepper, and sugar. Add the wine and simmer gently for about 10 minutes or until carrots are tender, adding a little water if they become dry. Remove the cover and cook at high heat until most of the liquid evaporates. Sprinkle with a little minced parsley and serve.

RED CABBAGE IN RED WINE

1 small head red cabbage, shredded
1 small onion, chopped
1 tart apple, peeled, cored and chopped
1 tbs. butter
1/2 cup water
1/2 cup dry red wine
1/4 cup grape jelly
Salt and pepper to taste

In a saucepan with a tight cover, bring the water to a boil and add all the ingredients except the jelly. Cover and cook until the cabbage is tender, about 30 minutes. Add the grape jelly and continue cooking for another 10 minutes. If there is too much liquid, pour it off into another pan, cook it down to about half, and add to the cabbage just before serving.

While this is an age of affluence it is also an age of overspent food budgets. Here is how to use more chicken in your menus. Use this good basting sauce for roast, oven-fried, or just plain barbecued chicken:

WINE BASTING SAUCE

1/4 cup red wine vinegar
1/2 cup dry white wine
1 cup chicken broth
1/2 tsp. oregano
1/2 tsp. rosemary
1 small clove garlic, crushed
2 tbs. onion, grated
2 tbs. honey
1 tsp. salt
1/2 tsp. soy sauce
1/2 cup corn oil
1 tbs. butter

Combine all the ingredients in a saucepan and heat just long enough to blend the flavors.

No doubt you have often wanted to serve a punch, but when you considered the cost of a bottle of good champagne, you hesitated. Now that you have a wine cellar full of good wines that cost you pennies instead of dollars, you can get out that punch bowl that has been gathering dust and have a ball.

LI'L OLE MOUNTAIN WINEMAKER WINE PUNCH

1 bottle Smoky Mountain Party Wine
1 bottle Wild Strawberry or Strawberry Rhubarb Wine
2 cups cranberry juice
1 pint fresh sliced strawberries
1 qt. bottle club soda

Have all ingredients well chilled. Set punch bowl in a bowl of cracked ice. Combine the first 4 ingredients; just before serving add the club soda. If not sweet enough, add a little sugar syrup.

For that chilly evening try this hot punch:

MULLED HARVEST MOON PUNCH

1 6-oz. can frozen pineapple juice concentrate
2 cups water
1 bottle Apple Wine
1/8 tsp. each of ground cloves and allspice
Sugar syrup to taste

Combine all ingredients. Heat slowly to just below the boiling point. Serve in preheated mugs with a cinnamon stick for a stirrer.

FOURTEEN

Have Fun

The purpose of any hobby is to employ one's leisure time doing something enjoyable — in other words, having fun. There are those who get so wrapped up in their hobbies that they cease to be fun and become plain work or drudgery. Ride your hobby but do not let it ride you.

Wine has been made and consumed and its virtues extolled as far back as recorded history. Good wine is not only pleasant to drink but acts as a relaxant. Wine is also a food that contains simple sugars, vitamins, minerals, and many enzymes. Many of the old-time medicines of the past had a wine base, and perhaps the wine was more beneficial than the other ingredients. Wine and food go together. Wine should never be served without the accompaniment of food.

Wine is a source of energy like any other food. The alcohol and sugar that remain in wine provide calories. Whiskey, on the other hand, composed of alcohol and water plus some coloring and flavorings, is practically all calories. Wine, in addition to the alcohol, retains many of the minerals and vitamins of the material from which it is fermented.

A small glass of wine before meals can act as an appetite stimulant, especially for the elderly. A little sweet wine at bedtime can act as a tranquilizer without any of the bad side effects of drugs. Wine with meals makes good food taste better. Try a glass of red wine with a bit of good cheese such as Gouda, cheddar, or blue.

I make no claim that wine can add years to your life. Oreste Di Tiburzio does, however, and he has the facts to prove it. He says he has found the secret to long life: "Don't drink water. It's not good for you."

Di Tiburzio should know — he has just celebrated his 100th birthday. He has a cup of coffee spiked with liquor to start the day. For lunch he has a glass of chianti, some fruit and a cookie. For dinner he has a boiled potato, a little meat, an egg, and more wine.

A boiled potato, a little meat, and a glass of wine add up to moderation. Here the secret of a long life is perhaps moderation along with the wine. Homemade wines have no chemicals in their makeup and have an alcohol content of about 10 to 14 percent by volume, so use them in moderation and you may live even longer than Di Tiburzio!

Traditionally, wine is served with meals. There are many more ways to use wine; it goes with any kind of function at just about any time of the day. A wine cooler, one-third water glass of wine, two ice cubes, and club soda or ginger ale, makes a delightful drink after any kind of exertion. Wine and cheese or wine and cookies for an unexpected guest or a new neighbor will break the ice of conversation and promote friendship. Most wines are served chilled, but there are times and occasions when hot wines are in order. At an outdoor party, around the barbecue pit on a chilly evening, a hot mulled wine is great. A light apple wine lends itself to this form of entertaining.

Wine is also traditional for the Christmas holidays entertaining and it can be used for any of the other midyear holidays as well. A Saint Patrick's Day party is lots of fun. Serve the guests, on arrival, Irish coffee and entertain with a buffet supper and several bottles of chilled wine or a wine punch. Wine punches are growing in popularity.

Last, and one of the best entertaining ideas, is a wine taster's party or a "What's My Wine?" tasting game. I recently attended a wine taster's party where the host entertained 24 guests. Ten wines were sampled. Each guest was given a sheet listing the wines and what to look for in judging them. Each guest later voted on the best all-around wine and the one with the best aroma and flavor.

After the party the guests were served spaghetti, corn-on-the-cob, and a salad. A small glass of a light dry blackberry wine was served with the dinner. It was a delightful evening and, in this age of so many tragedies on the highways, the host had the satisfaction of knowing that his guests were all capable of driving home safely.

The ideas put down here should only be the beginning of your wine education. There are many good books on entertaining and cooking with wine available at your wine supply store.

My parting advice is to have fun with the wine, no matter what the occasion.

Index